Developing Quality Practice Learning in Social Work

A Straightforward Guide for Practice Educators and Placement Supervisors

SECOND EDITION

By: Siobhan Maclean
with Ian Lloyd

Developing Quality Practice Learning in Social Work
A Straightforward Guide for Practice Educators and Placement Supervisors

First published 2008 by Kirwin Maclean Associates Ltd

First Edition 2008:		ISBN: 978-1-903575-51-2
**Second Edition 2013:		ISBN: 978-1-903575-88-8**

A catalogue record for this book will be available from The British Library

© *Kirwin Maclean Associates Ltd*
4 Mesnes Green
Lichfield
Staffs
WS14 9AB

All Rights Reserved
No Reproduction, copy or transmission of this publication may be made without written permission.

No paragraph of this publication may be reproduced, or transmitted save with written permission or in accordance with the provision
of the Copyright, Designs and Patents Act 1988.

Any person who does any unauthorised act in relation to this publication may be liable to criminal prosecution and civil claims for damages.

ISBN: 978-1-903575-88-8

Printed in Great Britain by 4edge Limited

Contents

Introduction 5

Understanding Social Work Education and Practice Learning 7
1. The Context of Social Work Qualifying Courses and Practice Learning 9
2. Post Qualifying Training and Learning: The ASYE 13
3. Language in Practice Learning 15
   Key Learning Points 19

Organising and Managing Practice Learning 21
4. Roles and Responsibilities 23
5. Off Site Placement Arrangements 27
6. The Practice Learning Process 32
7. Preparing for a Placement 37
8. Learning Agreements 41
9. Ground Rules and Boundaries 43
10. Ongoing Management of the Placement 46
    Key Learning Points 50

Facilitating the Student's Learning 51
11. Adult Learning Theory 53
12. Critical Reflection and Learning 63
13. Setting the Learning Agenda 69
14. Learning Opportunities 75
15. The Learning Environment 87
    Key Learning Points 89

Supervising the Student 91
16. An Introduction to Student Supervision 93
17. Functions of Supervision 98
18. Forms of Supervision 101
19. Practicalities of Student Supervision 103
    Key Learning Points 107

Assessing the Student 109
20. The Contemporary Framework for Assessment in Practice Learning 111
21. Using a Professional Framework 113
22. Holistic Assessment 117
23. Using Evidence in your Assessment 122
24. Professional Judgement and Assessment Decisions 127
25. Providing Feedback 129
26. Common Sources of Error in the Assessment of Competence 133
27. Completing the Assessment 136
    Key Learning Points 141

Values Issues 143
28. The Values Framework 145
29. Power and Practice Learning 148
30. Equality of Opportunity in Practice Learning 152
31. Ethical Issues in Practice Learning 156
     Key Learning Points... 158

When Things "Go Wrong" 159
32. Addressing Problems in Practice Learning 161
33. Working with Students in Failing or Marginal Situations........................... 163
     Key Learning Points... 167

CPD for Practice Educators 169
34. An Introduction to Professional Development 171
35. Continuing Development as a Practice Educator 173
     Key Learning Points... 176

References 177

INTRODUCTION

This reference guide has been written by experienced practice educators. The first edition was very widely used by those new to practice education but was also warmly received by those with existing experience in working with students. This new edition contains a range of practical suggestions about how to improve practice learning experiences. Recognising that many practice educators and supervisors using the guide will be working towards the Practice Educator Professional Standards, links are made to these throughout the text.

A practice educator's role is potentially vast. To enable us to cover all the information people may need, we have taken an approach based on the fact that practice educators potentially wear different 'hats' at different points of a placement. The three main 'hats' are:

MANAGER: The practice educator is responsible for the overall management of the placement

EDUCATOR: The practice educator is responsible for ensuring the student has access to appropriate learning opportunities and for facilitating the student's learning through the process of supervision

ASSESSOR: The practice educator is responsible for assessing the student and making a recommendation about whether the student has passed or failed the placement

These hats are essentially represented in the domains of the Practice Educator Professional Standards.

Where a practice educator is off site, they may share some of their 'hats' with the on site supervisor – more detail is given on this in Chapter 5.

Recognising these different hats, the reference guide has a number of sections covering some of the main aspects of a practice educator's role. Practice educators and supervisors should therefore be able to dip in and out of the book at the various points of a placement for hints and guidance.

It is important to see this publication as simply a guide. Practice educators and supervisors should develop their own unique and personal style, within the boundaries of good practice. In putting forward a range of ideas and suggestions, the reference guide seeks to give support to practice educators and supervisors in developing their own style of working.

It is also important to remember that different University programmes will have their own requirements in relation to practice learning and practice education.

The reader will therefore need to place the guidance provided in this publication within the context of the programme they are working with.

Working with students during their practice learning opportunities carries significant responsibilities. However, it should also be seen as a great opportunity to learn and to contribute to the future of the profession. We hope that this reference guide will help readers to meet their responsibilities and to get the most out of their experiences.

UNDERSTANDING SOCIAL WORK EDUCATION AND PRACTICE LEARNING

Social work education has changed significantly over the last few years. This section will help readers to develop their understanding of the current context of social work education and practice learning. A brief guide to the language and jargon involved in the field is included.

1 — THE CONTEXT OF SOCIAL WORK QUALIFYING COURSES AND PRACTICE LEARNING

Social work qualifying training has been at degree level since the autumn of 2003. Social work qualifying programmes can be taken at under-graduate level (generally leading to a BA) or post-graduate level (leading to an MA).

With continued momentum for reform and improvement (as a result of research, serious case reviews and public awareness) the Social Work Task Force (SWTF) was formed in 2009 by the Department of Health and the (then) Department for Children, Schools and Families (DCSF). The SWTF was made up of practitioners, educators and senior managers from across the profession, their remit was to undertake a comprehensive review of frontline social work practice and to make recommendations for improvement and reform of the whole profession.

By December 2009 the SWTF delivered its final report with 15 recommendations and as a consequence the SWTF was replaced by the Social Work Reform Board (SWRB) in 2010.

In 2012 the regulation of social workers and social work education in England was transferred to the Health Care Professionals Council (HCPC). At the same time social work education and training was reformed in a number of ways. The key reforms include:

- The introduction of the Professional Capabilities Framework (PCF) which now forms the basis for the selection of students, the design and delivery of the curriculum and the assessment of students
- The strengthening of partnerships composed of Universities, employers and service users and carers which work together to design and deliver course provision
- Work to improve the calibre of entrants to social work education
- Revised arrangements for practice learning
- New professional standards for practice educators

The regulation of social work qualifying programmes

As the regulator of social workers in England the HCPC sets standards for the education and training of potential social workers. Social work qualifying programmes are approved and monitored by the HCPC to ensure that they meet the required minimum standards.

As a regulator, the HCPC has a number of standards, which it is worth practice educators and placement supervisors being aware of:

Standards of proficiency: These standards apply to everyone on the register and also to students and those who want to join the register. They are minimum standards for safe and effective practice and include general elements as well as those specific to the particular profession.

Standards of conduct, performance and ethics: These standards only apply to those who are registered. However, students need to develop an understanding of these for when they do become registered.

Standards of education and training: These are the standards that an education and training programme must meet in order to be approved. These general standards make sure that anyone who completes an approved programme meets the standards of proficiency for their profession.

Professional requirements in social work qualifying programmes

As a regulator the HCPC does not set professional guidance – for example on the curriculum or entry standards. The College of Social Work carries responsibility for professional standards within social work qualifying education. The College describes its role as *"…on behalf of the profession, to promote good practice, provide information and guidance and disseminate research to support improvement in social work initial qualifying education."* (TCSW 2012: 5) As such, the College is carrying through a number of reforms to social work education first proposed by the Social Work Reform Board (SWRB) to improve the quality and consistency of the social work degree. These reforms have had a significant impact on the social work degree in the following ways:

Professional Capabilities Framework (PCF)

The PCF is a professional framework, which was designed with sector involvement. It provides a framework for professional social work practice across all areas of social work practice, at all stages of a social worker's career. This framework now forms the basis for the selection of students and the design and delivery of the qualifying curriculum. It also forms a key part of the criteria against which students are assessed. More information is provided on the PCF and the impact it has on social work education and training throughout this publication.

In general the College of Social Work (2012: 7) states that the PCF will:

- provide the basis for building an integrated, comprehensive and up to date curriculum
- provide a framework for four formal assessment phases during qualifying training: entry to the course, readiness for direct practice, end of first placement, end of last placement / qualifying level. At each point, efforts should be made to provide students not meeting the required standards with suitable exit routes
- clarify shared expectations of what is expected at the point of qualification
- improve overall consistency in curriculum design, delivery and assessment

Improving Partnership arrangements

The Social Work Task Force identified that Universities, students and employers of social workers had differing expectations about what social work graduates should be able to do at the point of qualification. These differences need to be addressed in social work education and therefore partnership arrangements have been strengthened in qualifying training. Universities, employers and service users and carers should work together to design and deliver course provision, working in line with the revised partnership arrangements.

Entry to social work education

The Social Work Reform Board stated that there was a need to improve "the calibre of entrants" to the social work degree. As a result there are revised requirements for entry to the degree programme, which can be summarised as follows:

Increased thresholds for entry: Academic requirements for entry have been increased.

Increased basic skills requirements: All applicants must have GSCE grade C or above in English and Maths or certificated equivalences, regardless of previous educational qualifications. All applicants must have the ability to use basic IT facilities, including word processing, internet browsing and use of email. Successful applicants must meet communicating and comprehension skills to International English Language Testing Systems (IELTS) at level 7.

Written tests: All candidates should complete a written test, regardless of previous qualifications or educational background.

Individual interviews: All candidates selected for the social work degree should have performed well in an individual interview to test their communication skills, motivation and commitment, understanding of social work and evaluation of their life and work experience.

Group activities: It is strongly recommended that observed group activities or exercises are used as part of the selection process.

Involvement of employers and service users and carers in selection processes: Employers and service users must be involved in the selection and interview processes.

Use of the PCF: The criteria for the selection of applicants for social work training is based on capability statements at entry level of the professional capabilities framework

The revised entry requirements are designed to ensure that candidates have *"the right mix of intellectual and personal qualities to succeed in professional training"* (TCSW 2012: 8).

Practice learning arrangements

The reforms to the social work degree require all programmes to have a consistent approach to practice learning. All students will have 200 days in practice learning which includes:

- 30 days for the development of practice and professional skills
- 70 days first placement
- 100 days last placement

Students are required to have different practice experience in the first and last placement. In the last placement they are expected to undertake tasks to prepare them for statutory interventions.

Professional standards for practice educators

The Practice Educator Professional Standards for Social Work were revised in 2012. They set out requirements at two defined stages and comprise outcomes that need to be met by practice educators working with students at different levels. The outcomes are laid out in four domains – which are referred to throughout this guide.

Practice educators who meet the requirements at stage one will be able to work with and assess students in their first placement, whilst those who meet the outcomes at stage two will be able to carry responsibility for the assessment of students in their final placement (at the point of qualification).

IN SUMMARY

Social work qualifying training has been at degree level for some years. In the recent past a number of reforms to social work education and training have been proposed. The College of Social Work are managing the implementation of these reforms which will have a significant impact on social work qualifying programmes and on the work of practice educators and placement supervisors.

2 POST QUALIFYING TRAINING AND LEARNING: THE ASYE

Chapter 1 covers the recent reforms to social work programmes. However, the Social Work Reform Board recommendations did not only cover social work qualifying programmes. The Reform Board also made significant recommendations about the continuous development of social workers beyond the point of qualification. One of the most significant of the recommendations related to the implementation of an assessed and supported year in employment for newly qualified social workers.

In March 2012 the Social Work Reform Board introduced this assessed and supported year in employment (ASYE) to replace existing NQSW programmes. Whereas NQSW programmes had been locally certificated and separated social workers working in children's services and adult services, the ASYE introduced a single programme to be certificated by the College of Social Work. The ASYE is based on offering newly qualified workers the opportunity to continue to develop their practice in their first year in employment. It is a year long programme during which newly qualified workers are expected to be supported to consolidate their learning from their degree studies.

Not all social work employers offer newly qualified social workers the opportunity of an assessed and supported year, but uptake is increasing. Newly qualified workers should expect the following in their first year in practice:

Learning agreement and personal development plan: newly qualified workers will complete a personal development plan and will develop a learning agreement with their employer which considers their experiences across the first year in practice.

Reflective supervision: supervision should be provided weekly for the first six weeks of employment, then fortnightly until the worker has completed six months in employment. Supervision should then take place at least monthly.

Workload: newly qualified workers can expect a 10% reduction in workload – such that they hold 90% of what would be expected of a worker in their second or third year in practice. This should be weighted over the year in terms of complexity and risk.

Protected development time: ordinarily equivalent to 10% over the course of the year should be allocated as protected time for personal development to enable the newly qualified worker to meet the needs identified in their personal development plan.

Holistic assessment: the newly qualified worker will be holistically assessed by a registered social worker against the PCF at ASYE level.

It is important for practice educators to be aware of the ASYE for two main reasons:

- At the point of completing the final placement students need to be clear about their development and where they still need to develop their practice. The further learning needs identified at the end of the final placement will be taken by the student into their first year in employment. Therefore it is important that practice educators support students to recognise that the end of the final placement is the beginning of a professional journey which will be supported by the ASYE.

- Whilst the requirements for the ASYE state that the worker needs to be assessed by a registered social worker many employers require newly qualified workers to be assessed by practice educators as they recognise the expertise that practice educators have in enabling progression and assessing performance. It is therefore likely that practice educators will be asked to become involved in some aspect of supporting or assessing newly qualified workers on the ASYE.

IN SUMMARY

The implementation of the ASYE is seen as a key aspect of the social work reform programme. It is important that practice educators understand the ASYE and recognise the ways in which they can contribute to a newly qualified social worker's experiences.

3. LANGUAGE IN PRACTICE LEARNING

Language is a very powerful tool and a good understanding of language is very empowering. For many people new to practice education, practice learning appears to have a language all of its own. If you have ever been to another country where you didn't understand the language, you will understand how difficult it is to find your way around. Many students, practice educators and others involved in practice learning feel that way in their first experiences of practice learning. This reference guide should equip you with the information you need to find your way around. This chapter begins that process by giving some basic information on the words, phrases and abbreviations you may come across. More detailed information is to be found in the remainder of this guide.

Abbreviations

Abbreviations are perhaps what most of us think of when we hear the word "jargon". Abbreviations tend to be put together as a form of shorthand but they can be one of the most dangerous forms of jargon. What one person believes an abbreviation to stand for may not be the same as another person's understanding.

As a practice educator or student supervisor, you will quickly develop an understanding of how many abbreviations you use in your working practice. Students are likely to be confused by the range of abbreviations used in the placement setting – many workers are unaware of how much jargon they use until a student comes along and asks questions about it! As someone new to practice learning, you will probably be able to empathise with a student, as you become confused by the amount of jargon involved in practice learning.

Some of the more common abbreviations you will come across in practice learning follow:

ALS	-	Action learning set
APEL	-	Accreditation of Prior Experience and Learning
APL	-	Accreditation of Prior Learning
ASYE	-	Assessed and Supported Year in Employment
BA	-	Bachelor of Arts (Degree)
BASW	-	Bachelor of Arts in Social Work (Degree)
BSc	-	Bachelor of Science (Degree)
BSocSc	-	Bachelor of Social Science (Degree)
BTec	-	Business and Technology Education Council
CPD	-	Continuing Professional Development
CQSW	-	Certificate of Qualification in Social Work (replaced by DipSW)
DipSW	-	Diploma in Social Work (replaced by the Social Work Degree)
DO	-	Direct Observation
DoH	-	Department of Health
EAL	-	Enquiry and action learning
EPD	-	Early professional development

FE	-	Further Education
GCSE	-	General Certification of Secondary Education
HCPC	-	Health Care Professionals Council
HE	-	Higher Education
HEI	-	Higher Education Institute (University)
HNC	-	Higher National Certificate
HND	-	Higher National Diploma
IASSW	-	International Association of Schools of Social Work
IELTS	-	International English Language Testing Systems
IFSW	-	International Federation of Social Workers
LAPT	-	Long Arm Practice Teacher (now outdated – long arm is replaced by off site)
LSI	-	Learning Styles Inventory
LSQ	-	Learning Styles Questionnaire
MA	-	Masters Award (Post Graduate Award)
MASW	-	Masters in Social Work (Post Graduate Award)
MPM	-	Mid placement meeting
NOPT	-	National Organisation for Practice Teaching
NQSW	-	Newly Qualified Social Worker
OSS	-	On site supervisor
PA	-	Practice assessor
PAP	-	Practice Assessment Panel
PBL	-	Problem based learning
PCF	-	Professional Capabilities Framework
PE	-	Practice Educator
PEPs	-	Practice Educator Professional Standards
PIVs	-	Private, independent and voluntary sector
PLO	-	Practice learning opportunity
PLOpp	-	Practice learning opportunity
PMG	-	Programme Management Group
PPM	-	Pre placement meeting
PQSW	-	Post Qualifying Award in Social Work
PT	-	Practice teacher
PTSG	-	Practice Teacher Support Group
QAPL	-	Quality Assurance of Practice Learning
SETs	-	Standards of Education and Training (HCPC standards)
SOPs	-	Standards of Proficiency (HCPC Standards)
SSC	-	Sector Skills Council
SURG	-	Service User Reference Group
TCSW	-	The College of Social Work
WBA	-	Work Based Assessor

Words and Phrases

You may come across a whole range of terms, words and phrases which are new to you when you enter the world of practice learning. As you work through this guide, these should be clarified for you. This chapter clarifies some of the words used and explains why we have chosen to use some terms rather than others.

Practice Educator

In this edition we have chosen to use this as our preferred term. Although this phrase has been around for some time now, when we wrote the first edition we used the term practice teacher as it was the most commonly used term across England at that time. The term 'Practice Teacher' is still in use and sometimes the term 'Practice Assessor' is used. However, there is significant criticism of both titles, as they emphasise either the 'teaching' or 'assessing' role, rather than showing how both are included. You may, however, hear all three phrases used to describe the same role. We feel that practice educator is a term which demonstrates both the assessment and learning roles held by the person who has overall responsibility for the placement.

Placement

This is the word used to describe the time a student spends in practice as part of their social work training.

Some Universities use the term practice learning opportunity rather than placement. A range of language is used around placements or practice learning opportunities:

- placement provider: a term used to indicate the agency providing the practice learning opportunity
- host team: the team providing the learning opportunity
- placement agency: the agency/organisation offering the practice learning opportunity
- practice learning site: the location of the placement
- integrated placement: integrated placements are where students are placed in a variety of settings to maximise opportunities – they can be organised around particular issues or particular service user groups
- split placement: another term for an integrated placement
- network placement: another term for an integrated placement

Programme

Essentially, the word programme refers to the course the student is undertaking. All social work courses are managed by the University but they must involve partners (or Stakeholders – see below) in the design, delivery and evaluation of the programme.

Stakeholders

A number of groups are seen as stakeholders in the delivery of social work training. The word partners or stakeholders is used to describe these groups. The key 'stakeholders' in social work education are seen as:

- Employers
- Higher Education Institutes (Universities)

- Students
- Service Users and Carers
- Practice Educators
- External Examiners

A range of other words and phrases are used in practice learning – the remaining sections of this guide will introduce, define and clarify these as necessary.

IN SUMMARY

Language which is new to people can be very confusing. Students may find the range of language and jargon used in placement settings confuses them and it is important that they should feel comfortable in seeking clarification. This section has introduced some of the language and jargon used in practice learning. It's important to have a clear understanding of the language used – practice educators and supervisors should act as a role model to students by seeking clarification about language which is new to them.

KEY LEARNING POINTS

- Social work qualifying training is at degree level
- The degree in social work is made up of University based learning and practice learning
- There have been significant changes to the Social Work degree in England in recent years
- Continual Professional Development is vital for social workers
- Practice educators need to have an understanding of the ASYE
- For those new to practice education, it can feel as though it has a language all of its own

ORGANISING AND MANAGING PRACTICE LEARNING

One of the key roles of a practice educator is to manage the placement to ensure that the student has effective learning opportunities such that they are able to develop their practice and demonstrate their capability. In order to effectively manage the placement, a practice educator needs to have a good understanding of a range of issues. This section therefore covers the roles and responsibilities of those involved in practice learning; the process of practice learning; preparing for a placement and agreements around practice learning.

4 ROLES AND RESPONSIBILITIES

There are potentially a huge number of people involved in the provision of an effective placement. Many people consider that there are three key players in each social work practice learning situation – the student, the practice educator and the tutor. To some extent this is true – however, we consider that the host team and the team manager also have key roles.

Increasingly students are placed in practice learning environments where there is no practice educator on site. In this situation, a student will work with a supervisor who is on site and an off site practice educator will work with the student and supervisor. In this situation, the on site supervisor has a particularly important role. Off site arrangements are discussed in more detail in Chapter 5.

In this section, the role and responsibilities of the practice educator, the student, the host team, team manager and the tutor are covered. It is important to remember that different programmes may have some particular requirements in terms of these roles. However, what follows is a general outline of the usual expectations in terms of roles and responsibilities.

Practice Educator

The practice educator may also be called a practice assessor or practice teacher. They are responsible for the overall management of the placement and as covered on page 5, wear several different 'hats' at different points in the placement.

In more detail, the practice educator role and responsibilities generally includes:

- Management Aspects
- Preparation of the team and the agency more generally for the placement and for the particular student
- Liaison with other agencies, other professionals and team colleagues to ensure effective opportunities and support for the student
- Ensuring that the student has access to and adheres to relevant policies and procedures
- Taking responsibility for the co-ordination of events in the case of any concerns arising during the placement
- Attendance at relevant meetings relating to the placement – usually a pre-placement meeting, mid placement meeting and possibly a final placement meeting
- Ensuring appropriate cover in their absence
- Ensuring accountability arrangements are clear and that effective line management is in place
- Ensuring that the student has access to essential equipment (eg: telephone) and that they have a place to sit and work etc.

Teaching Aspects

- Developing an effective learning agreement and learning curriculum
- Arranging an appropriate induction pack and induction programme for the student
- Identification of appropriate learning opportunities
- Ensuring the student receives all necessary learning opportunities
- Providing structured supervision sessions for the student on a regular basis – generally weekly or fortnightly
- Providing necessary informal supervision, advice and guidance to the student
- Supporting the student to develop practice skills
- Supporting the student to link University based learning to their practice on placement. For example, linking theory and practice, law and practice, values and practice etc.

Assessment Aspects

- Direct observation of the student's practice
- Provision of feedback to the student about their practice
- Liaison with other relevant people to gather feedback about the student's practice
- Judging the evidence provided by the student against the assessment criteria
- Writing reports in relation to the student's progress on placement. Generally a mid placement report and a final placement report
- Making a recommendation about whether the student has passed or failed the placement
- Marking any work produced by the student during the practice learning opportunity as may be required by the programme
- In the event of concerns that the student may be failing or marginal, instigating relevant concerns procedures

Where the practice teacher is off site, these responsibilities will be shared with the on site supervisor (see Chapter 5).

The Student

Students take responsibility for their own learning; it is as much their responsibility to make the placement a success as any other participant. It is important that the student is aware of this from the outset of the placement.

The Student should:

- Attend all relevant placement meetings
- Be open and honest about their learning needs and highlight these at the learning agreement meeting
- Take responsibility for their actions whilst engaged in the placement and learning opportunities provided
- Adhere to agency policies, procedures and guidelines
- Be pro-active in the placement. For example, in seeking out appropriate learning opportunities
- Identify where they believe their learning needs are not being met during the course of the placement

- Integrate with the host team appropriately
- Identify with the practice educator poor practice and forms of oppression and challenge appropriately with the required support
- Be prepared to challenge their own thinking and those of others where appropriate and safe to do so
- Be pro-active in preparation for supervision sessions
- Identify appropriate opportunities for direct observations of practice
- Provide evidence of their practice
- Produce any academic work relating to the practice learning opportunity as required by the particular programme

The Tutor

The Tutor's responsibility lies predominantly within the academic setting. However the tutor has a fundamental role in the negotiation of the learning agreement, and the process of the placement.

The Tutor should:

- Contribute at the pivotal points of the placement, ie: placement agreement, mid point review, final placement meeting
- Provide tutorial support to the student in relation to any academic work that has to be completed during the placement

In the case of any concerns about the placement or about the student, the tutor should be contacted and they will have a role to play in any concerns procedures.

The Team

The importance of the team being effectively involved in the provision of the placement cannot be under-estimated. The members of the team hosting the student's placement hold the key to the experiences that the student will learn from. Their involvement will ensure that the student experiences what it is like to work in teams.

The team therefore, needs to be "on board". Dysfunctional teams or teams which do not want to host a placement will impact significantly on the potential success of the placement.

Team members should:

- Be welcoming to the student and support them to integrate into the team
- Be willing to provide learning opportunities for the student – such as allowing the student to shadow their practice
- Be willing to provide feedback about their views on the student's practice to the student and practice educator
- Identify any evidence they have about the student's practice and share this with the student and practice educator
- Highlight any concerns as early as possible

The team manager should:

- Ensure the practice educator has sufficient time and practical facilities to undertake their role effectively
- Ensure that team members play their role in the placement
- Ensure that any work which is allocated to the student is appropriate to their student status

The role that a team plays in a practice learning opportunity can make or break the placement and the experiences of the student and the practice educator. If the team is not fully "engaged" the practice educator's role will be particularly difficult.

IN SUMMARY

There are a number of people involved in the provision of a placement and each of them has a distinct role to play.

5. OFF SITE PLACEMENT ARRANGEMENTS

In some situations teams which are willing and able to provide a practice learning opportunity for a social work student have no one on the team who can act as a practice educator. This is becoming more common with the increasing diversity in practice learning environments. In these situations, a supervisor will be nominated from within the team and a practice educator who is based somewhere else will work with the student. The term used for this is off site arrangements. Hence the practice educator is termed an off site practice educator whilst the supervisor is known as an on site supervisor, work based supervisor or job supervisor. The language previously used was "long arm" – a long arm practice teacher (LAPT). However, this is now recognised as potentially oppressive to some people with disabilities and is generally seen as an outdated term.

We have also heard off site arrangements called tandem arrangements. This explains the system well – the practice educator and on site supervisor work in tandem to provide a good quality practice learning opportunity for a student.

There are various advantages to off site practice learning arrangements:

- The student has two people providing support. This gives them access to a broader range of experiences
- As the practice educator works off site, they will not be involved in office or team politics and can provide an objective "sounding board" for the student to discuss their experiences of working as part of a team
- The off site practice educator's time for practice learning should be "ring fenced" so the student can be sure they receive the time they need.

However, these advantages will only be maximised if the arrangements are clear and the practice learning opportunity is well managed. The key to this is ensuring that relationships are clearly negotiated.

It is helpful to view the key relationships in off site arrangements, using a triangulation model as follows:

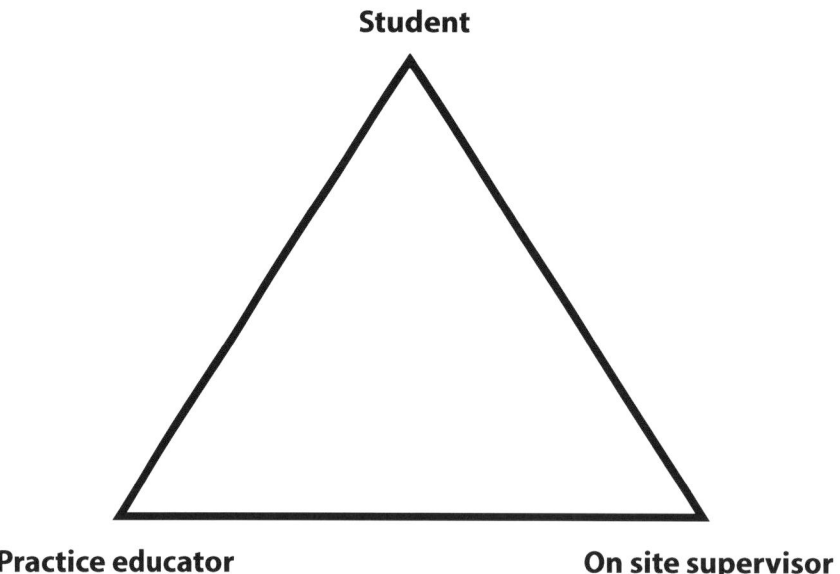

As can be seen from this representation, it is important for each of the three key players in the placement to have a close working relationship to the other two.

Our experiences indicate that at times, the relationship between the practice educator and on site supervisor is not always well developed. In many situations the triangle looks more like:

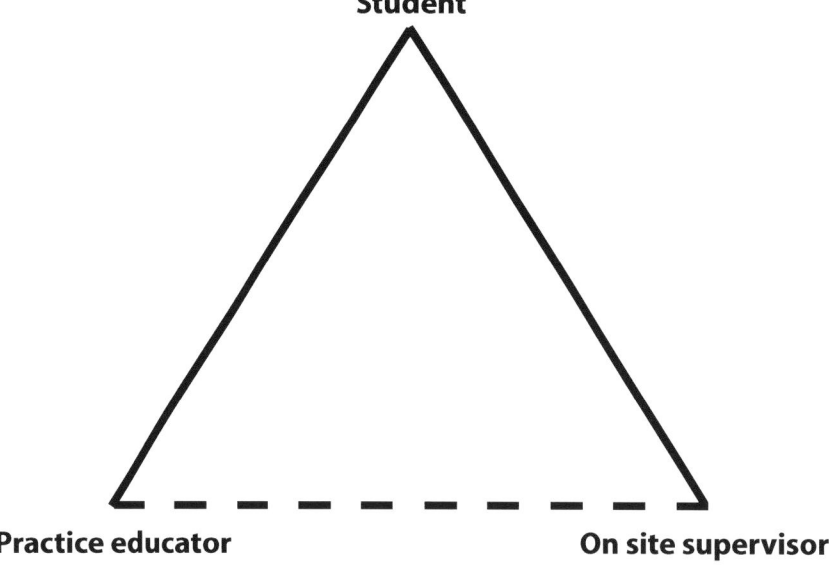

Using a visual image, it is clear that in the above representation, the triangle is not so solid. Both practice educator and on site supervisor are working effectively with the student but because they are not working effectively and closely together, then the support offered to the student is not as "stable" as it could be.

Where the practice educator and on site supervisor do not clearly negotiate their working relationship, this can lead to confusion for the student, practice educator and on site supervisor. Further, it can mean that host teams are not willing to offer further placements in the future.

Negotiating the Relationship

There are no hard and fast rules in off site placements. The key to every off site situation is good communication between the on site supervisor and practice educator.

Atherton (2006:21) asserts that in off site placement arrangements "there are two clear and precise areas of accountability" as indicated in the following diagram:

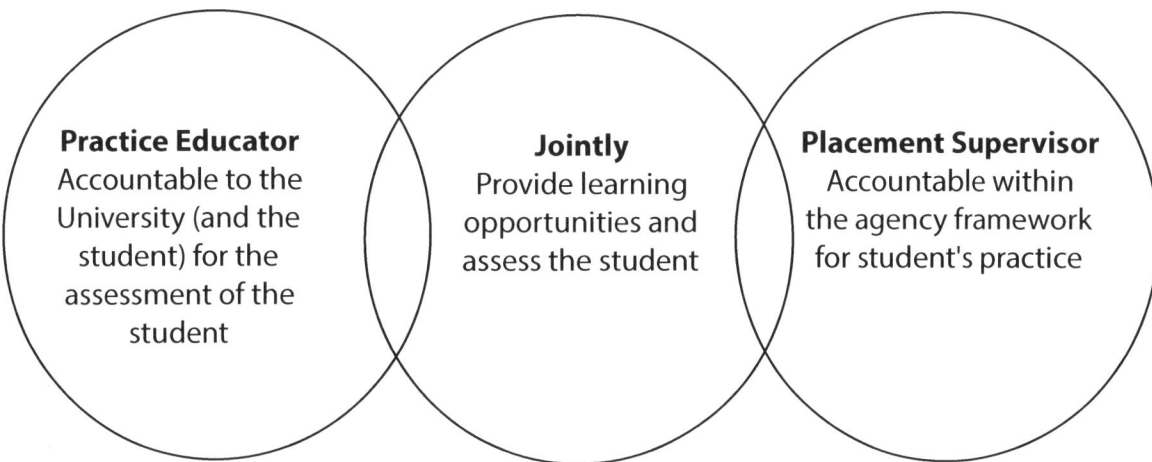

In off site placement situations we find that the best starting point for negotiating arrangements is to think about all of the tasks that would need to be undertaken by an on site practice educator and then negotiate the division of these between the off site practice educator and the on site supervisor.

In every off site situation, the way in which the relationship works and the way that the tasks are divided will be different. The key to a successful placement is clear negotiation prior to the start of the placement about who will do what, when and how. This should be regularly reviewed during the placement and should be open to change as necessary.

It is useful to develop some notes for use in your negotiations. This helps everyone to be clear about who will do what and when. Copies of the completed notes should be shared with all involved. Remember to provide a copy for the student – this helps clarify roles for them too.

The following framework might be useful in helping you to develop notes for negotiations about off site arrangements:

NEGOTIATING RESPONSIBILITIES

Task	To Be Carried Out By		Notes
	Practice educator	On site Supervisor	
♦ Placement Profile			
♦ Preparing the team			
♦ Ensuring practice resources (eg: desk)			
♦ Informal meeting with the student			
♦ Attending pre-placement meeting			
♦ Writing learning agreement			
♦ Preparing induction pack			
♦ Devising induction programme			
♦ Devising learning curriculum			
♦ Supervision: Formal			
♦ Supervision: Informal			
♦ Allocation of work			
♦ Direct observations of student's practice			
♦ Obtaining service user feedback			
♦ Obtaining colleague feedback			
♦ Mid-placement report			
♦ Attending mid-placement meeting			
♦ Writing final report			
♦ Attending final placement meeting			
♦ Contributing to placement evaluation			

Exactly who does what will depend on a range of factors including how much the on site supervisor wants to do, the nature of the practice learning opportunity, the experiences of all involved etc.

As a general guide, we find that tasks which require an in-depth knowledge of the practice learning environment (the team, local agencies etc) are best carried out by the on site supervisor with advice and support from the practice educator. This would include tasks such as devising the practice learning profile, planning the induction etc. On the other hand, specific practice learning tasks are usually best carried out by the practice educator with feedback and support from the on site supervisor. This would include tasks such as devising the learning agreement, the learning curriculum and writing the placement reports. Other tasks may need to be carried out by both the on site supervisor and off site practice educator – for example, both should attend meetings about the placement.

The key issue is the provision of supervision. This is always a tricky one to negotiate. The on site supervisor will always be the one to provide the day to day informal supervision that the student will need – they are the one that will be there in the agency when the student has questions etc. Regular, formal supervision must always be provided by the practice educator – as this is the main forum for their education and assessment roles. However, outside of these basics, supervision responsibilities can be blurred. Since the on site supervisor is accountable for the work carried out by the student, they will also need to carry out some formal supervision in line with agency policy. The danger is that if supervision isn't clearly negotiated, the student may feel "over supervised". They may find they are repeating themselves, covering the same issues in two separate supervision sessions. To address this, some practice educators and on site supervisors arrange occasional joint supervision sessions where both attend – these generally only include both on site supervisor and off site practice educator for half of the session and then the practice educator and student have half the session alone. This can work really well in some situations but in other situations, a student may be overwhelmed or feel overpowered. So it is vital to negotiate very carefully with the student and keep this under review.

One other area which is vital for practice educators to discuss with on site supervisors is how concerns will be addressed. Any anxieties which on site supervisors might have will be heightened unless there is clarity about the following points:

- How will any concerns they have about the student's practice be addressed?
- How will any concerns the student might raise about the agency/practice learning setting be addressed?

Each University programme should have guidelines about what action would be taken in each of these circumstances. It is important to clarify these and ensure that everyone involved is informed about possible arrangements.

IN SUMMARY

Essentially, in off site placement arrangements, the role of the practice educator is divided between two people. However, the off site practice educator retains overall responsibility for managing the placement.

It should be clear from this chapter, that the key to making sure off site practice learning arrangements work, is clear communication and a clarity about roles and responsibilities.

6 THE PRACTICE LEARNING PROCESS

Whilst it is important to remember that each social work programme will differ in terms of specific requirements, placements generally follow a broad pattern. The following practice learning process diagram can be adapted and used to ensure that all necessary steps in planning and delivering an effective placement are followed.

This chapter gives a brief outline of each stage of the process. More detail is given in the remaining sections of the guide.

PRACTICE LEARNING PROCESS

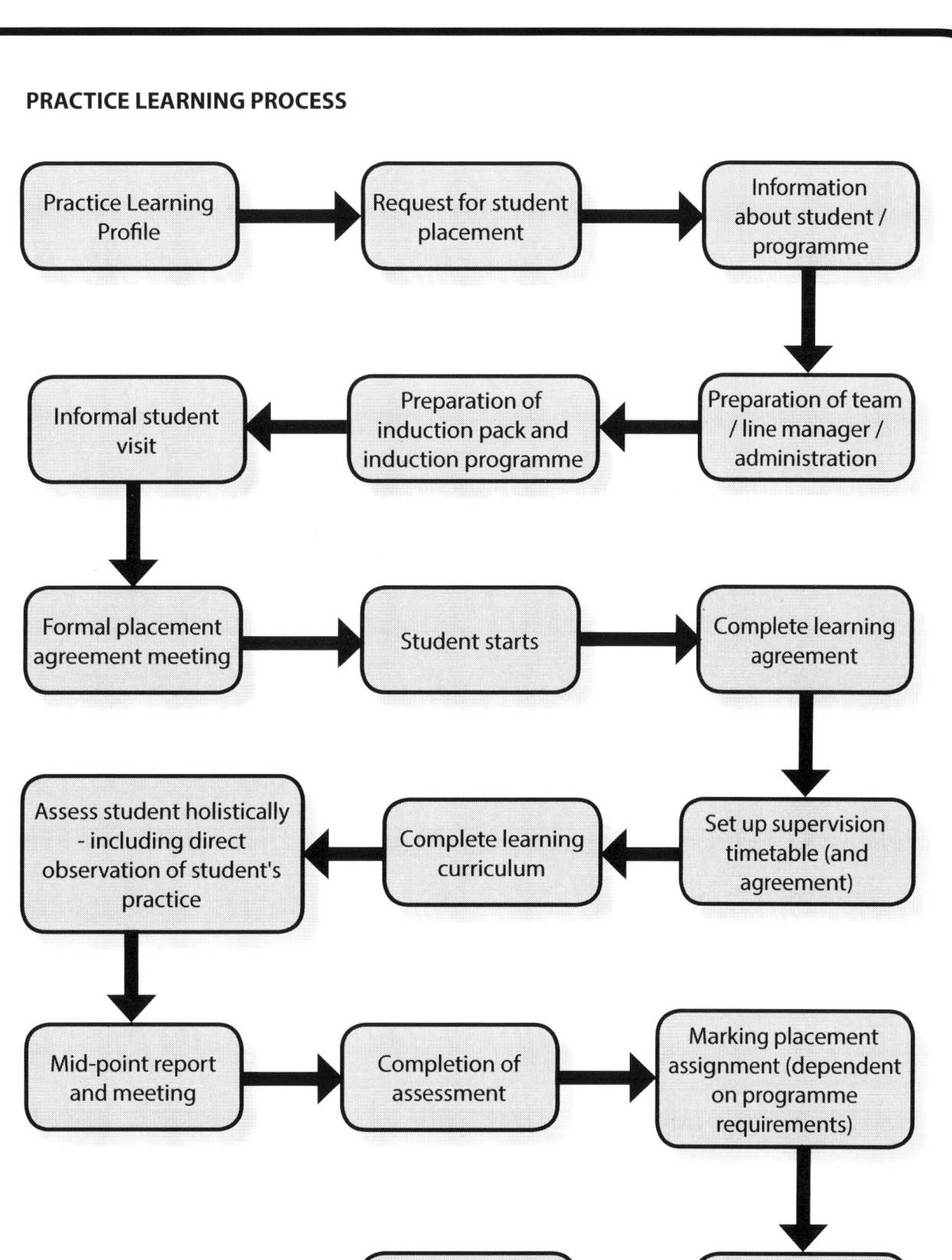

NB It is important to remember that programmes vary in terms of requirements - eg: paperwork requirements etc. This process may therefore need to be adapted depending on particular requirements

Practice Learning Profile

A practice learning profile should be completed in as much detail as possible by the practice educator – possibly involving the team manager. It should contain information about the team, local community and resources, the building and opportunities available. It is a key tool in the matching process where students and practice learning opportunities are matched. It can be passed to the practice learning co-ordinator at the University or in the placement agency who will undertake the matching with care. They should be able to advise what to include and should be able to provide examples of completed profiles to help with this task. See Chapter 7 for more detail on practice learning profiles.

Team Preparation

The relevant practice learning co-ordinator will contact a practice educator with a request for a student placement. At this point, potential host teams should obtain information about the student and their programme. Ask to see copies of any previous placement reports and a copy of the programme handbook. This will help you ascertain if you can meet the learning needs of the student. If you are happy to proceed – say no if you are not – begin the preparation of the team. Teams need, as a minimum, to have an understanding of the social work student role, the HCPC standards of proficiency, the PCF, course requirements, learning opportunities and the roles and responsibilities of all involved. The team will need to have a positive outlook and be able to support the student and practice educator. Team meetings are a useful place to start these discussions and begin addressing any concerns or misunderstandings.

Team members are crucial to making a placement a success. They not only provide learning opportunities but contribute to the overall assessment of the student. See Chapter 7 for more detailed guidance on preparing the team.

Student Induction

Generally, students need to know about the purpose and policies of an agency. They need to learn about practices of the agency e.g: signing in/out, have the opportunity to meet key people, observe experienced workers and begin to develop a sense of their role within the team and the wider agency.

It is likely that your team has an existing induction pack and possibly a standard induction programme and many teams use that as a basis for designing student induction arrangements. However, it is very important that this is specifically tailored to the needs of a student social worker. See pages 76-79 for more detail on induction processes.

Meetings with the Student

Informal meeting
An informal student visit should take place before a formal practice agreement is made. At the informal meeting the student, practice educator and team need to have time to discuss expectations and opportunities. This meeting should be arranged by the student. It is very important as it is a genuine chance for any potential problems to be highlighted and addressed.

At this point, if either the student or the practice educator feels that there are potential difficulties which cannot be addressed, the practice learning opportunity may not go ahead.

Formal meeting

Once it is agreed that the placement will go ahead, a formal meeting will take place. This is sometimes referred to as a pre-placement meeting, a contract meeting or a learning agreement meeting. At this meeting a contract, often referred to as the practice learning agreement, is drawn up. This formalises arrangements and the aims of the placement. The meeting is attended by the student, practice educator (and supervisor if applicable) and usually the tutor. This meeting is a further opportunity for potential difficulties within the placement to be identified. Realistically it is much harder for any party to withdraw at this stage.

It is good practice for this meeting to take place before the student actually starts the placement. However, in practice and in line with some Higher Education Institute's requirements, sometimes this meeting is held in the first or second week of the placement. It is important that it is no later than this since the learning agreement is a key document in ensuring that all parties are aware of the student's needs and the roles and responsibilities of everyone involved.

Ensure that you make full use of the meeting and the negotiation of the learning agreement to clarify any concerns or confusion and to establish clear lines of communication. What is expected of you will be made clear – take the opportunity to clarify what you expect of others. See Chapter 8 for more details on learning agreements.

Supervision

Once the student has started, supervision arrangements should be established. The practice educator should devise a supervision agreement and possibly a supervision "timetable" with the student. Supervision is explored in detail in Chapters 16-19.

Planning the Learning

The practice educator will often, in conjunction with the student and relevant others, draw up a learning curriculum. The style of these can vary but essentially they are a plan of the student's learning which will identify what learning opportunities the student will have and who is responsible for providing them. Most will include review dates and provide a way of ensuring the student's needs are kept at the forefront of the learning opportunity. See Chapter 13 for more detail on learning curriculums.

Assessment of the Student

As the placement proceeds, the practice educator and student will work together to ensure that evidence of the students practice is gathered. This includes direct observation of the student's practice. See Chapters 20-27 for more information about assessing a student.

Some students, however, do fail to provide evidence that they are capable and competent. If the student is felt to be failing the placement, then the practice educator should contact the student's tutor and a "concerns" meeting is likely to be called. Different programmes have different procedures for dealing with failing or marginal students. If this becomes an issue, you must seek advice from the student's tutor. See Chapter 33 for more information.

Mid Point Review Meeting

The mid point meeting, often referred to as the mid placement meeting is a formal meeting involving the student, tutor, practice educator and supervisor (where relevant).

It is essentially an opportunity to review the placement and in particular the student's progress. Some Universities require brief reports at this stage. At this stage of the placement the meeting and report provide an important opportunity to identify any strengths, consider any difficulties and agree future learning needs and the focus for the remainder of the placement.

Completion of Assessment

In the final stages of the placement the assessment must be completed. The student should complete their portfolio and the practice educator will complete their report. It is a requirement that service users are involved in the assessment of the student and the practice educator and student must facilitate this. Some programmes will require the practice educator to mark student placement assignments. The practice educator is responsible for making a recommendation of pass or fail. See Chapter 27 for more information.

Placement Assignments

The majority of social work programmes require students to write at least one piece of academic work about their placement experience – this may be a case study or an analysis of an aspect of their practice. Sometimes practice educators will be involved in the marking of these. Where Universities involve practice educators in marking assignments or in formally marking a student's portfolio, they will provide guidance and/or training on this.

Final Placement Meeting

The final placement meeting with the student is a chance to reflect on the placement and learning opportunities provided. The practice learning opportunity should be evaluated by the student, team and practice educator. This stage sometimes gets overlooked. However, it provides an important opportunity to learn from the placement, improve it for future students and acknowledge the work of all involved. It is helpful to also have a debrief meeting with the team where possible to further acknowledge the work of those involved.

Providing practice learning opportunities can be immensely rewarding for a team and the individuals involved, but providing a placement is a significant piece of work. Recognising this and providing feedback helps ensure placement host teams feel valued and are more likely to embark on the role again. See page 48 for guidance on placement endings.

IN SUMMARY

There is a clear process to practice learning. Whilst this may need to be adapted in terms of particular programme requirements or specific agency issues, it is useful for practice educators and supervisors to have a clear understanding of the process of practice learning.

7 PREPARING FOR A PLACEMENT

This is undoubtedly the most important aspect of a successful placement. Remember the 4P rule:

> Poor Preparation will lead to a Poor Placement

Preparation prior to the decision to offer a placement will certainly build the odds in favour of a success.

Deciding whether to offer a placement

Some points to consider in deciding whether to offer a student placement follow. They are only suggestions, but they are tried and tested and have proved very useful in ensuring quality in all aspects of the process of a placement.

- Can the team facilitate and accommodate a student's learning?
- Is the team manager interested in supporting the accommodation of a student?
- Are the team resources and networks happy to accommodate a student's learning?
- Can you commit appropriately to a student's learning?
- Have you got contingencies in place where you are on leave or absent from work to facilitate a student's learning?
- Do you have colleagues who are willing and able to step in when you are unexpectedly absent from work, to continue facilitating a student's learning?

If you are confident about your ability to provide an effective practice learning opportunity for a student, you can then begin to prepare effectively.

Practice Learning Profiles

Many programmes require a profile to be sent to the relevant practice learning co-ordinator to ensure an effective match between student and placement. Profiles are also useful to provide to the student during induction. Some programmes also require profiles to be attached to learning agreements. So whilst it may seem like another extra task to complete a profile at this stage, it will be time saving in the long run. Once a profile has been produced, it will only need to be updated as each new practice learning opportunity is due to begin.

Many programmes will have their own pro forma and guidelines on what should be included in a practice learning profile. However, the following guidelines may help practice educators when devising a practice learning profile:

AGENCY PROFILE

- **Location:** eg: rural, urban, demography of local community, accessibility for students (transport), housing, and size of area covered by the team etc.

- **Building:** What is access to the building like? Who else shares the building eg: agency teams, other agencies?

- **Office routine/facilities/practicalities:** Office arrangements (open plan or private), access to desk, telephone, admin support, car parking, tea fund etc.

- **Local resources:** both agency and independent eg: nurseries, hospitals, day centres, groups etc.

- **Team issues:** composition, management and where located, experience etc.

- **Social work opportunities:** what opportunities will be available to the student?

- **Methods of assessment available:** what methods will be used to assess a student?

- **Other information:** Some practice learning sites are considered only suitable if a student has their own transport etc. Here you should give any information deemed relevant but not yet covered.

In addition to agency profiles, personal profiles are also important in preparing for a placement. Again, these can be useful to provide to students during induction and some programmes ask for personal profiles to be attached to learning agreements.

As a minimum, a practice educator and on site supervisor should produce a personal profile. Other team members may also wish to provide a personal profile.

PERSONAL PROFILE

- Professional qualifications
- Background and experience
- Areas of expertise and interest
- Gender
- Racial origin: this may be particularly important information to a student who may be seeking to work with a practice educator from the same origin as themselves

There are a range of advantages to completing a profile at this stage. As previously stated, this will be time saving to you in the long run. The process of completing the profiles can also help you to see what action you might need to take to accommodate a student in the office, what limitations there may be in terms of what you can offer and what team preparation may need to be done. In short, the process of completing profiles will prompt reflection about necessary preparation.

Preparing the Team

Wherever a student is placed, practice learning is not just about the practice educator and student. The team on which the student is placed has a vital part to play and the practice educator must give careful consideration to preparing the team for their role effectively.

In off site situations, the on site supervisor and off site practice educator should negotiate who will be responsible for each aspect of the preparation of the team. The following guidance is by no means exhaustive but has been developed by a group of experienced practice educators and will be helpful when considering team preparation.

- Allow sufficient time to prepare the team before the placement begins. Involve the team in all aspects of practice learning. Share information and keep the team up to date.
- Develop a team exercise/strategies to:
  - identify team skills
  - identify experience
  - identify strengths
  - identify any team/individual learning needs
  - reassure team members
  - establish the importance of having students and the positive gains made by the team from social work practice learning
- Establish:
  - team support
  - line manager support
  - admin and support staff support (where relevant)
- Clarify the role, issues and expectations of:
  - student
  - practice educator
  - on site supervisor (where relevant)
  - team colleagues
  - tutor
- Negotiate/clarify areas of responsibility around areas such as:
  - who allocates work to the student?
  - what kind of feedback is required by the practice educator and how will this be facilitated?
  - who is available for informal supervision and support?

- Nominate another person in the team as back-up for the practice educator or on site supervisor
- Make the student aware of the team's involvement
- Develop a knowledge of the team culture and informal rules eg: tea making, message system, accepted behaviours etc.
- Share the student's learning needs with the team. Discuss how the team can be involved in providing learning opportunities and feedback
- Prepare the team for the pro-active stance/ "challenge" of the student in all areas, particularly in terms of values and anti-oppressive practice. Questioning is part of the student role and needs to be seen as a learning opportunity and not as a threat to the team or individual team member
- Encourage the team to draw on the student's knowledge and skills. Questioning and learning is a two way process

It is vital that the team is well prepared for the placement, particularly that they understand the role of the practice educator, the role of a student social worker and the role of an on site supervisor where applicable.

IN SUMMARY

Our experience indicates that where things go wrong in practice learning (at any stage) it often relates back to a lack of preparation before the placement actually begins. As you have reached the end of this chapter, you should take some time to reflect on the practice learning environment, your experiences, your team and wider links with other colleagues and put some thought into what you may need to do to prepare effectively for your work with a student.

8 LEARNING AGREEMENTS

In terms of managing the placement, the learning agreement is probably the key document. Sometimes called a placement agreement, a learning contract or a placement contract, this should be negotiated and agreed by the student, the practice educator, the on site supervisor (if relevant) and the tutor. Some Universities expect the student to complete the agreement, some expect the tutor to complete it and some expect the practice educator to complete it. Whoever actually writes the agreement, it should be negotiated, agreed and signed by all involved. Each person should have their own copy.

A formal meeting should be held just before the placement starts or just after it has started. This is the ideal time to negotiate the learning agreement. Most Universities provide a pro forma which simply needs to be completed to form the agreement. However, these vary significantly from one University to another. Our advice would be to check any learning agreement pro forma against the following guidance which was originally offered by the National Organisation for Practice Teaching (NOPT, 2006) on what should be covered in a learning agreement.

Where the practice educator (and supervisor) have prepared effectively for the placement, the agreement should be fairly straightforward to negotiate. The programme handbook is also vitally important as this will detail the University expectations of the placement.

It is not unusual for people to see the completion of the learning agreement as simply a 'paper exercise' which needs to be completed to meet agency and / or University requirements.

However, not only is the agreement a key document, the discussion and negotiation that takes place in completing the agreement is vitally important in setting the context of a placement.

The most effective practice education focuses on student's directing their own learning. When students are self directing, practice educators can focus on facilitating growth and promoting factors are consistently highlighted as promoting self-directed learning:

- establishing a climate that is conducive to learning
- the learner being actively involved (and leading where possible) all stages of the learning process

These factors can be fully addressed in negotiating a learning agreement, hence promoting self-directed learning from the very start of the placement.

The guidance provided by NOPT on what should be included in an agreement is useful. However, we would also include something on ground rules which would include issues such as the use of mobile phones in the working environment, agency expectations with regards to dress etc. Some students come to placement with very limited previous experience and may need some support and advice on professional expectations. It is useful to ensure that these are discussed, agreed and recorded within the learning agreement at the outset of the placement.

It is important that the learning agreement is used as a working document throughout the placement. It should not be written and then put to one side. Keep arrangements under review and make amendments to the agreement where necessary.

LEARNING AGREEMENTS

- Contact details of all those involved
- Profiles of student, agency, tutor, practice educator and supervisor, as needed
- Health and Safety factors
- Information about the student's previous practice learning
- Particular learning needs of student
- Learning opportunities linked to learning outcomes
- Frequency of supervision
- Expectations for supervision including recording and teaching methods
- Involvement of people who use services in the learning process
- Arrangements for direct observation of practice
- Assessment methods
- Profile of expectation for academic work, marking of assignments etc
- Student access to administration support
- Hours of work, sickness/absence policies of both the practice learning site and the Higher Education Institute
- Arrangements for ongoing support, teaching and assessment in the absence of the practice educator
- Student access to:
    - agency in-house training
    - learning resources
    - agency support systems for example, occupational health
- Student access to student support group in agency or locally
- Arrangements to resolve disagreements
- Dates of mid placement review, final placement meeting/submission of assessment report etc
- Student access within the academic setting to student support services

(NOPT 2006)

IN SUMMARY

A clearly negotiated, comprehensive learning agreement is a key document in setting up the placement and managing the learning opportunity.

9 GROUND RULES AND BOUNDARIES

It will be clear from what you have read so far that clarity about ground rules and boundaries in practice learning is essential. The successful ongoing management of a placement will rely on clear ground rules and boundaries so we felt it worth devoting a chapter specifically to this area.

Ground Rules

You will know that part of negotiating learning and creating an effective learning environment is being clear about ground rules. Whenever you go on any training course, you start with agreeing ground rules. In a practice learning environment, ground rules are essential. With more and more students coming into practice learning without any previous professional experience, ground rules are even more vital – no ground rule can be left "unwritten", no assumption can be made that students understand what we might consider to be obvious professional ground rules – these are only obvious to people who have been working for some time. So spend some time with students early in the placement agreeing ground rules around areas such as:

- confidentiality - what exactly do we mean by this?
- appropriate challenging - how should a student expect to be challenged? How might they go about challenging others?
- professional behaviour
- expectations with regard to dress
- use of mobile phones
- relationships with team members
- relationships and boundaries with service users
- use of the internet at work
- use of social networking and social media
- working hours, breaks etc

This list is not exhaustive but gives some idea of the kinds of areas you should discuss. Invite the student to highlight any ground rules they would like added. Ensure the ground rules are revisited as the placement progresses.

Atherton (2006) states that:

"Ground rules directly reflect social work values and this can be made explicit in setting them up."

She goes on to discuss the experiences of practice educators in agreeing ground rules with students:

"Those practice educators who adopted ground rules felt that the process of discussing ground rules was useful in itself – perhaps more important than the result."

(Atherton 2006:36)

Whilst it could seem that discussing ground rules in this way could exaggerate power differentials, we feel that a partnership based approach to agreeing ground rules actually helps in promoting a safe learning environment since a student is clear what expectations there are. Do make sure though that it's not a matter of "one rule for you and another for me". You must work within the ground rules agreed too!

Boundaries

Similar to ground rules, but perhaps more specific are issues of boundaries. Issues of boundaries can be difficult for students in relation to a range of areas – for example, what boundaries there should be to their relationships with colleagues and relationships with service users? Doel and Shardlow (2005) recognise this and have produced an excellent exercise for use with students which helps explore some of the ethical issues around boundaries in terms of professional relationships with service users.

It is our experience that sometimes boundaries in practice learning relationships can become blurred – this is generally in relation to the practice educator/student relationship but could extend into relationships between students and team members and other relationships in practice learning. Essentially, the relationship between the student and practice educator (and supervisor where relevant) is a professional relationship and professional boundaries should be in place. Where these boundaries are blurred, it will certainly create problems between students and practice educators/supervisors should any difficulties be encountered along the way. Imagine, for example, how difficult it would be to objectively assess a student where a friendship has developed – or even more complex, how you could fail a student if they consider you, and you consider them, "a friend".

Getting the balance right is difficult. You are not a friend to the student, you have a job to do (a practice educator or supervisor) and that forms the basis of your relationship. However, neither do you want to appear too clinical or cold towards a student. To ensure you have the balance right, think through some of the following areas, decide where your boundaries will lie and discuss these boundaries and the reason for them with the student and others who may be affected (eg: team colleagues).

Will you:

- Give a student your home or personal mobile phone number?
- Tell a student your address?
- Go to a student's home?
- Talk to the student about their personal circumstances?
- Invite a student on a staff night out?
- Invite a student to a team "pub lunch"?
- Lend money to a student?
- Lend books to a student?
- Accept a present from a student?
- Talk about your personal circumstances to a student?
- Go to a party hosted by a student?
- Invite a student to a party hosted by you?

Practice educators, supervisors and teams often find boundary issues problematic so it really is worth thinking these through before the start of a placement. Discussing these issues in a team meeting can be really helpful and enlightening.

There is no real right or wrong answer to whether you would do some of the things we have raised in these questions. However, we find that where they have been discussed, boundaries tend to be clearer and more robust.

This is not to say, of course, that boundaries can't change when the relationship ends. I am now good friends with many of the students I have worked with in the past. While the placement is in progress, however, you have an assessment relationship with the student and this must be considered in the boundaries of your relationship.

Forming an effective learning environment

Chapter 15 explores the concept of the learning environment. In many ways we see the establishing of ground rules and boundaries as creating the basis for an effective learning environment. Thinking visually, the ground rules create the foundations of the learning environment, whilst the boundaries build the walls - this creates a 'built environment' in which the student is clear about their learning and effective relationships can develop without misunderstandings.

IN SUMMARY

Ground rules and professional boundaries are an essential aspect of all social work practice. This is no less so in practice learning. Ground rules and boundaries should be carefully negotiated at the outset of the placement and kept under review.

10 ONGOING MANAGEMENT OF THE PLACEMENT

Thorough and effective preparation for practice learning is essential, but effective practice learning management needs to continue throughout the whole course of the placement. The role of a practice educator has been referred to as similar to the role of a conductor working with an orchestra (Hughes 2006). This is a clear analogy in that there are potentially a huge number of people involved in any practice learning opportunity (the orchestra) and it is the practice educator's responsibility to manage or co-ordinate everyone's input into the placement (the conductor).

A quick consideration of who might be involved in the provision of a placement and who might have an impact from the "edges" shows the number of people involved:

```
        admin staff
                            practice assessment panel

service users
                                        tutor
                        student                  team manager

        team colleagues

                    on site supervisor        practice educator

    other professionals

                        other students
                                            practice learning
                                            co-ordinator
```

You will know from your practice experience, that collaborative working involving this number of people is potentially problematic. People will have differing agendas, differing views, a variety of policies and procedures directing their work etc. All of this can mean that the 'orchestra' of practice learning supporting a student could be very out of tune. In order to 'conduct' the practice learning opportunity effectively, the practice educator needs to manage the input of all involved. Certainly effective preparation will help with this, but the management role needs to continue throughout the placement. The subsequent sections outline aspects of the teaching and assessing roles of practice educators. Following the guidance contained in these sections will assist in managing a practice learning opportunity. Other essential aspects of managing a placement include:

- *Power*
  It is essential to be aware of the power dynamics inherent in practice learning relationships. Chapter 29 gives more detailed information on the power dynamics in practice learning. You will know that power differentials have a significant impact on relationships and effective partnership working. In order to effectively co-ordinate the involvement of everyone involved in the placement, it's important to work sensitively with these power dynamics.

- *Open Communication*
  It is vital that there is clear and open communication between all involved in the placement. To facilitate trust, another vital aspect of managing the placement, all communication between players should be openly shared with all involved.

- *Listening*
  It's vital that practice educators employ all of their communication skills – particularly their active listening skills. Practice educators need to truly listen to all involved throughout the placement. For a number of reasons students, team members and on site supervisors (where applicable) may not raise any concerns they have directly with a practice educator. Here it is vital that the practice educator makes full use of their active listening skills – "the practice educator has to take the initiative and try to pick up clues". (Atherton 2006:24)

- *Boundaries*
  It's vital that boundaries are clarified from the outset and kept under review. This means clarifying the boundaries of relationships, the boundaries of the student's role and that of others etc. See Chapter 9 for more information on boundaries.

- *Partnership*
  Everyone involved in social work and social care should be aware of the importance of working in partnership with people who use services and with other professionals. Practice educators and supervisors should employ their skills in working in partnership to ensure that the learning experience is student focussed and that everyone works in partnership to maximise the student's opportunities and to make the placement a positive experience.

- *Awareness of Process and Procedures*
  In order to effectively manage a placement, practice educators and supervisors should have an awareness of the practice learning process, the expectations of all involved etc. They also need to be aware of key policies and procedures of both the agency and the University – for example, it is important to be aware of concerns procedures, whistleblowing policies, complaints procedures etc.

- *Monitoring and Reviewing*
  Arrangements in practice learning should be kept under regular review. Practice educators should monitor placement arrangements and the contributions of everyone involved. Any amendments to arrangements should be negotiated between all concerned and recorded.

Placement Endings

Managing a placement effectively also involves ensuring smooth placement endings.

For a range of reasons, it is important that thought is put into placement endings. Very significant time and energy is put into placement preparation and establishing the student in the placement. This is vitally important, as has already been covered. However, it is also important to devote some time to effective endings. This is vital if the host team is to offer placements to other social work students in the future.

A final placement meeting generally takes place between the student, tutor, practice educator and on site supervisor (where applicable) and this should facilitate an effective ending for the student. However, it is also important that the team are supported in placement endings. As such, it is helpful for the team to hold a meeting (or devote part of a team meeting) to debrief about the placement. This is particularly important if there have been any difficulties in the placement.

The debrief will cover issues such as what went well. It can be useful to use the following "agenda" to cover pertinent issues:

- Surprises - what, if anything, surprised the team?
- Satisfactions - what were the team satisfied with?
- Dissatisfactions - is there anything which team members were dissatisfied with?
- Learning - what were the main learning points of the placement for the student? Team members should be invited to say what they learnt from the student or from the placement generally.

(adapted from University of York, 2000)

Practice educators and supervisors should contribute fully to the team debrief – what surprised you? What did you learn? etc. Obviously there will be some discussions about the specific student, their needs, their progress etc but we find that using this agenda helps to bring out more general issues which will help improve the placement for future students.

It is important to remember that where there have been difficulties within a placement – for example, significant conflict, a failing or marginal student etc., a more significant debrief will be needed. Host teams should not be left to deal with these issues alone.

Placement Evaluation

It is important that every placement is fully evaluated. Students, tutors, practice educators and supervisors should all be involved in evaluating the placement. This is not about the student, but is about evaluating the quality of the placement, the opportunities provided, and the practice learning provision in general.

Universities generally use the quality assurance benchmark statement and evaluation tools for practice learning, which are commonly referred to as QAPL (Quality Assurance for Practice Learning). The QAPL framework was revised in 2012 and is widely available on the internet.

Practice educators and supervisors should use this opportunity to receive feedback on the practice learning environment and on their skills. Learning from the evaluation should help the practice educator and supervisor (where relevant) to improve the placement and their own skills for the future.

IN SUMMARY

Managing the placement is about a range of issues being taken into account. It continues throughout the practice learning opportunity and involves the practice educator ensuring smooth endings for all involved.

KEY LEARNING POINTS

- It is essential to be clear about the roles and responsibilities of everyone involved in a placement and to communicate clearly about these

- Off site practice learning arrangements are becoming more common

- The key to effective off site arrangements is a clearly negotiated relationship between the on site supervisor and off site practice educator

- Different Universities have different requirements but there is a clear process to practice learning

- Placement preparation is vital - if effective preparation does not take place, the placement probably won't go well

- The learning agreement is a vital tool in terms of the effective organisation and management of practice learning

- A key aspect of the practice educator's role is managing the input of all involved in practice learning

- Ground rules and boundaries are an essential aspect of organising and managing the placement

- Practice educators and placement supervisors often see the organisation and management role as being about the very start of the placement. However, these issues continue throughout the placement

- Practice learning should be carefully evaluated - generally the QAPL framework is utilised to evaluate and quality assure

FACILITATING THE STUDENT'S LEARNING

Some people become anxious about being an 'educator'. They think they need to get out a chalk and board and "teach" a student. Whilst there may be a place for some teaching about specific placement issues, a practice educator does not have to be proficient with a chalkboard (or even an interactive whiteboard!) The teaching aspect of the role is much more about facilitating a student's learning. A student should have learnt, through their time in University, about key aspects of social work. The practice educator's role is essentially about supporting the student to apply this to practice and to facilitate the student's learning about practice environments.

11 ADULT LEARNING THEORY

In order to effectively facilitate a student's learning, it is important to have an understanding of the main theories and principles of adult learning. These should guide your practice in facilitating the student's learning.

Basic Principles of Adult Learning

- *The Law of Exercise*

Adults learn best when they take part in the activity they are learning about. Unless they have the experience within the environment where it is normally practiced, then they may not learn the task completely. The law of exercise basically says that the more opportunities a person has to engage in an activity, the more they will learn about it. Practice makes perfect sums it up really!

- *The Law of Association*

Adults learn best by adding to, or building on, previous knowledge. If we have already had an experience and we have a similar or related experience, then we stand a better chance of learning from it. The more we can 'associate' new experiences and learning with something we are already confident with, the more likely we are to learn from the new experience.

- *The "need to know" motivation*

Adults always learn something more effectively if they want to or need to learn it. The attitude of "what's the point?" will render us less likely to learn or retain the learning. This may mean that sometimes you need to advise a student why they need to learn something in order to make their learning more effective. This principle is one of the reasons that I tend to work on a What? Why? How? basis to facilitating learning. Working through the questions, what do you need to be able to do? Why? How can you develop these skills? is a useful approach to take in facilitating learning.

- *The need to be self-directing*

Adults need to take responsibility for what they learn. We learn best when we are directing our own learning. Many of the processes in practice learning build on this principle – for example, asking students to identify their own learning needs and expecting them to engage fully in devising the learning agreement and learning curriculum.

- *The readiness to learn*

Linking in with the self directing principle, if someone is not ready to learn and puts up barriers or obstructions, then no matter how good the experience of learning or the quality of the teaching or facilitation, the person will not be able to learn effectively.

- *Learning empowerment*

If the relationship between the practice educator and the student is seen as one where the practice educator is the full container and the student is the empty container, the full value of the information will not be realised. The student needs to have a confidence that they are able to learn from the experiences undertaken, not by being given an account of the experiences. All professionals in social care should be familiar with concepts of empowerment; these should be employed in facilitating learning.

- *The learning environment*

The situation in which we learn is paramount, we need to feel safe to learn, we need to feel confident to learn. Practice educators and supervisors should work to create a safe learning environment for the student.

- *Plateau learning*

We have all heard the phrase "a steep learning curve". We learn in peaks and troughs, we will have days when we learn more than others, and some days where we feel we are not learning anything new at all. Having time and space to consolidate learning before taking on new learning is important. Learning curves all need to plateau at some point. Students may need some reassurance during these times.

- *Learning continuum*

Adults continue to learn throughout their lives. We need to recognise that we never stop learning and it is imperative never to believe that we cannot learn any more.

- *Positive learning*

If we receive positive reinforcement about a subject or learned experience, we are more likely to remember or learn from it. This reinforces the need for positive constructive feedback to facilitate learning.

Theories of Adult Learning

A range of adult learning theories are particularly useful in relation to practice learning. This chapter covers some of the key theories which practice educators and supervisors may find useful in facilitating a student's learning.

Experiential Learning

This theory is sometimes misinterpreted as simply saying that people learn through experience. To some extent this is true but experiential learning theory asserts that it's not enough for people to have an experience – they won't learn from this unless they spend some time reflecting on the experience.

Perhaps the most well known academic to write about experiential learning is Kolb (1984). He states that people need to go through the following cycle in order to learn.

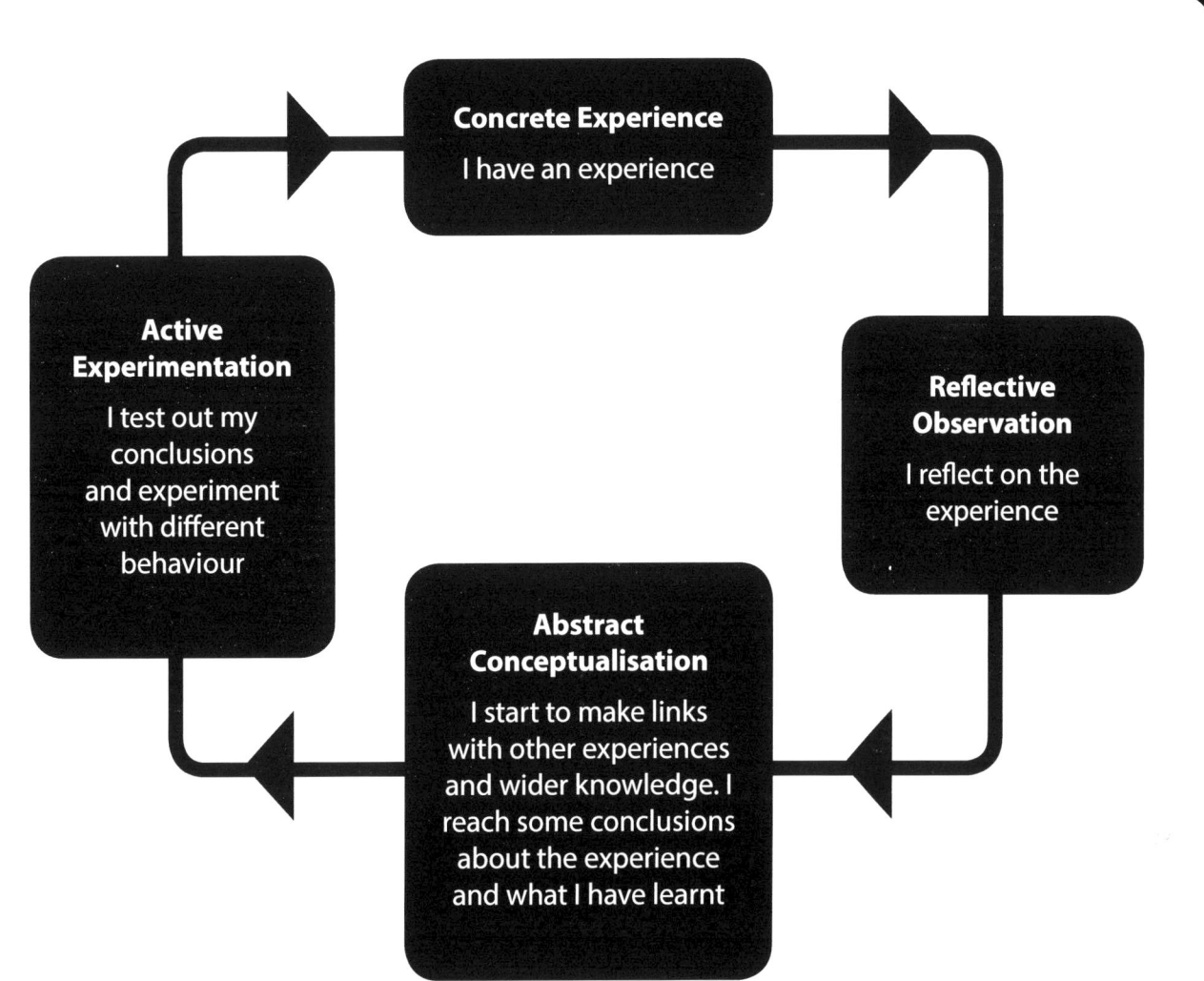

This theory of adult learning is particularly helpful as a practice educator, as it clearly demonstrates that it's not enough to simply immerse a student in a range of experiences. They won't necessarily learn from the experience unless they are supported to follow through the learning cycle in supervision discussion. This is where what is commonly referred to as a coaching conversation comes in.

To support a student to go around the learning cycle fully, a practice educator can:

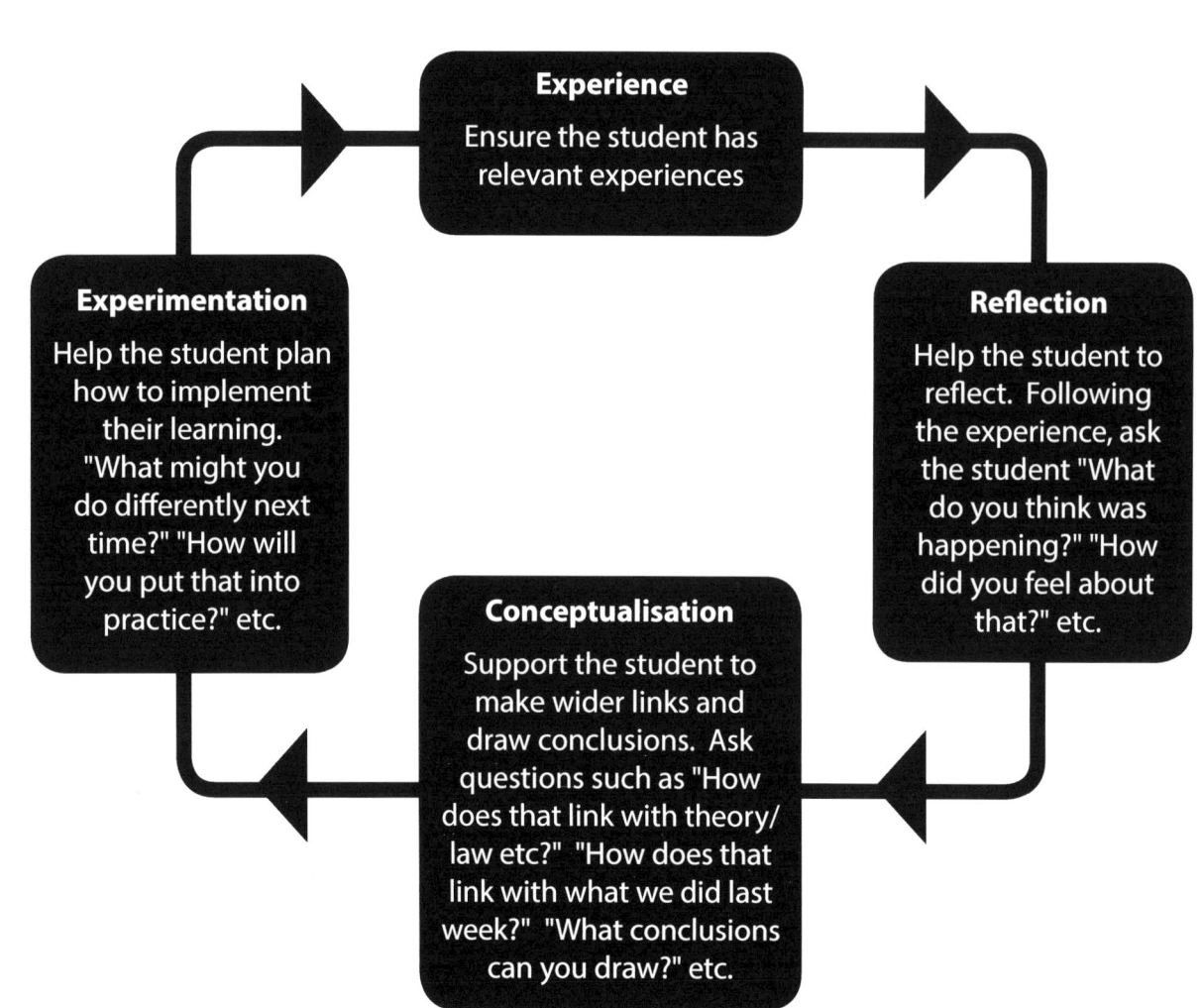

As a practice educator you may find that students get "stuck" at certain parts of the learning cycle. For example, a student may be able to reflect on their experience and draw conclusions about what they might want to do differently next time, but then they appear to repeat mistakes. They may be getting stuck at the "active experimentation" phase. Here you will be able to make use of the coaching conversation and concentrate your questioning and discussion in this area.

Humanist Learning Theories

Developed from the work of Carl Rogers (eg: 1980) this is sometimes referred to as facilitative learning. Opposing behaviourist approaches which see learning as a consequence of extrinsic (external) rewards, humanists argue that learning is a result of intrinsic (internal) rewards. The approach is based on the belief that people have a natural eagerness to learn and that people will learn in order to meet their needs for self actualisation. Self satisfaction is the motivating force for learning. Humanistic approaches are linked to the idea that adults are self directing in their learning.

A number of specific theories are drawn out of the humanistic approach. For example, Burns (1995: 233) argues that andragogy is "very much in the spirit of the humanist approach to learning and education."

Andragogy

Malcolm Knowles (1978) believes that most adult teaching has consisted of teaching adults as if they were children. He argues that adults are different from children as learners in three critical ways:

1. *In terms of their self concept.* Whereas a child first sees themselves as a completely dependent personality, the adult has developed a concept of themselves which values a certain degree of autonomy. Adults have a need to be perceived as self directing. The deepest need an adult has is to be treated as an adult, to be treated as a self directing person, to be treated with respect.

2. *In terms of their experience.* Whereas a child defines his or her self identity by reference to their family, school, community etc. Adults usually define themselves in terms of their experiences. Self identity is derived from what we have done. Accordingly adults are very jealous of the worth of our experience and wherever we find people devaluing our experience, not paying attention to it, not incorporating it in the education plan, we feel rejected as people.

3. *In terms of their time perspective.* Whereas in most aspects of life, a child's time perspective is one of immediacy they find it hard to postpone the satisfaction of present desires, an adult is more accustomed to postponing immediate satisfactions. But in regard to learning, the time perspectives of children and adults is reversed. Children become used to learning things that will not have immediate application, but will be accumulated into a reservoir of knowledge and skills that will/may be useful in adult life. But an adult's perspective in regard to learning is likely to be one of immediate application. According to Knowles the reason an adult enters into education is to be able to better deal with some life problem about which they feel inadequate now.

Knowles refers to the approach of teaching children as pedagogy and says that the teaching of adults should be based on a different approach which he calls andragogy. Andragogy should take account of the differences outlined above.

Situated Learning Theory

The whole concept of practice learning is based on the idea of situated learning theory – a term coined by Lave in the 1980s. He argues that learning needs to take place in the context and culture in which the activity ordinarily occurs (ie: where it is situated). Social interaction is an essential aspect of situated learning. Learners need to become involved in a "community of practice". As the learner moves from the edge of this community to its centre, they become more active and engaged in their learning. Lave and Wenger (1990) call this process "legitimate peripheral participation". Lave and Wenger carried out an analysis of situated learning involving professionals in five different settings (including midwives). In all five cases, they found that learners had a gradual acquisition of knowledge and skills as they learnt from 'experts' in the context of everyday activities. Others have further developed the concept of situated learning. Brown, Collins and Duguid (1989) emphasised the idea of "cognitive apprenticeship".

Clearly, practice learning links closely to theories around situated learning. What can be drawn from this theory is the importance of involving whole teams in placement activities with the student – making the most of opportunities for the student to be included in the "community of practice".

Cognitive Dissonance

This is a theory drawn from psychology and used widely in understanding people's behaviour, motivation etc. It was first written about by Leon Festinger (1957). The theory is that people feel a sense of dissonance when there is conflict between their attitudes, beliefs or behaviours.

People find the dissonance uncomfortable (potentially painful) and so they seek to alter the beliefs, attitudes of behaviour to reduce the discomfort and restore the balance. Sometimes the person's attempt to maintain 'cognitive consistency' rather than experiencing cognitive dissonance can lead to seemingly irrational or maladaptive behaviour. We find understanding that dissonance can create unexpected behaviours particularly useful in understanding some students responses to learning. It works particularly well when viewed in conjunction with the ladder of learning, as follows:

The Ladder of Learning

This is a longstanding model used in understanding learning. There is significant debate about the origins of the model and it is attributed to many writers. We use it in understanding how cognitive dissonance can be created during a learning process.

The idea is that we all go through four phases when we are called on to learn something new:

1. *Unconscious Incompetence*
   When asked to undertake a new task, we don't know what we don't know. It could be said that we're incompetent but that we are unconscious of this. In a way this is quite a comfortable stage – it could be seen as "blissful ignorance". We don't know that we can't do something. However, as we attempt to undertake the new task, we quickly realise that there is a lot more involved than we think and we move onto:

2. *Conscious Incompetence*
   Now we become aware of what we don't know – we realise that we can't do the new task. This is a very uncomfortable and potentially painful stage. Many people are socialised to believe "there's no such word as can't" and becoming conscious of our incompetence is distressing. This can create a situation of cognitive dissonance. This is created because the learner needs to do something which they don't feel able to (so there is a potential conflict between their beliefs "I can't do it" and their actions - doing it).

   At this phase, some people decide to concede the learning – give up on the task. People can develop quite sophisticated defence mechanisms to ensure that people around them aren't aware of their "incompetence". Think of the highly developed systems that some adults with literacy difficulties have developed.

   Others seek out support and new and useful experiences in order to get through this stage, learn the task and move onto the next stage:

3. *Conscious Competence*

   When we have recently learnt a new task we are very aware or conscious about it. Think about that new driver who is saying "mirror, signal, manoeuvre" every time they go out in a car! Whilst we may be anxious to ensure we get things right, this is probably the most comfortable and safe stage to be in. We are aware of what we are doing so we are likely to continue to question ourselves and are probably getting it right! The danger is that we will probably, at some point, move onto the next stage:

4. *Unconscious Competence*

   This is where we have become so familiar with the task and confident about our abilities that we almost go onto an "automatic pilot". The potentially dangerous aspect of this is that when we are unconscious about something, how do we know that we are still doing it right? Think how many of us (if we are honest) wouldn't pass our driving test today if we just had an examiner sitting in the car on one of our usual journeys. When we are unconscious about something, we slip into bad habits, we take shortcuts – maybe we have actually slipped back to the phase of unconscious incompetence. If we are unconscious, how do we know? That's one of the main joys of being involved in practice learning – students ask a range of questions which help you to keep your practice under review – maintaining consciousness about your practice.

Having an understanding of the way that cognitive dissonance can be created during the learning process is very useful in practice learning. You will be able to acknowledge the additional support students may need in phase two. Where students may avoid a task etc because they are uncomfortable at stage two, you will be able to recognise this as an aspect of learning as opposed to think they are lacking in motivation etc. We certainly wouldn't suggest using this by saying something like "Don't worry – you're incompetent and you're just realising that. You'll get through it." That certainly wouldn't help a student's confidence, but having an understanding of the process of dissonance yourself can be very helpful.

Learning Styles

Honey & Mumford (1982) report that people have different styles of learning. They have developed four different styles and have designed a learning styles questionnaire which identifies which style a person uses. These questionnaires are widely available in social work practice learning. This is a very interesting exercise to use with a student at the start and the end of a placement because there is also a suggestion that we can adopt new styles during a specific learning period due to the way in which fellow learners, or the facilitator of the learning, influences how we learn. Some Universities ask students to complete a learning styles questionnaire (sometimes referred to as an inventory) at various stages in the course so students may be familiar with this exercise.

The four learning styles identified by Honey and Mumford are:

<u>Activists</u>

Activists are often open minded and enthusiastic; they like new experiences and want to get involved in the here and now. They enjoy getting involved and they learn by "doing". Activists can become bored when an activity stops and will want to quickly move onto the next challenge or activity, rather than dwell on reflection of the last activity.

Reflectors

Reflectors (do just what it says on the tin!) they stand back, reflect, ponder and consider many perspectives before acting. Reflectors mull over things before reaching a conclusion; they observe, gather information and use plenty of time to think things over.

Theorists

Theorists are logical thinkers; they analyse, question and learn step by step in a logical way. Theorists question any new learning and want to ensure it fits and makes sense with their logical approach. Theorists are often perfectionists and don't appreciate a flippant approach to a subject.

Pragmatists

Pragmatists like to try out something new to see if it works in practice. They will often take a problem solving approach to learning and will seek to apply something that they have learnt straight away. However, if it doesn't work they are likely not to try the approach again – instead they will try to look for something new to try.

As a practice educator, it is useful to have some understanding of these identified styles and approaches. However, it is important to remember that these are a theoretical approach. They are not scientifically set and it is vital to remember that there are other influences on how an adult learns.

Approaches to Learning

Although they are most well known for devising learning styles, Honey and Mumford (1986) also assert that there are four different approaches to learning. These are different to the styles of learning they discuss. In practice learning, references are often made to learning styles and less commonly to approaches to learning. However, we find an understanding of approaches to learning very useful in practice education. The approaches identified are as follows:

Intuitive Learning

We are not conscious of this, but we are learning by our experience; if we use the intuitive approach then we are making use of the experiences we have to learn and develop. If this approach is challenged we are able to refer to a variety of detail of experiences. However if questioned, the intuitive learner finds it difficult to articulate what they have learnt or how they have learnt it. People who are intuitive learners regularly see themselves as having attended the University of Life! Intuitive learners tend to think they learn through a process of osmosis - simply soaking in what goes on around them.

The Incidental Approach

This generally involves learning by chance from activities that force an individual to carry out a reflection of the situation. This can sometimes be borne out of frustration. If something happens to an incidental learner, for example something in their plan goes wrong, they will often reflect over the incident in an unstructured informal way.

This can happen in less formal patterns; travelling home, sitting in the garden or even lying in the bath. Incidental learners often use the "benefit of hindsight" as a way of rationalising what has happened.

Incidental learners will often discuss their experience with someone else; it is even more beneficial to discuss it with someone who was present at the time of the experience.

The Retrospective Approach

Similar to the incidental approach, the retrospective learner looks back over what has happened and then goes on to draw a specific conclusion from it. However, people using this approach will also tend to draw lessons from routines and successes. So in effect, they are learning from a diverse range of small and large, positive and negative experiences.

The process looks something like this:

The Prospective Approach

This is similar to the above, except that there is another dimension included; this is the dimension of planning. The experience is planned for, set up and then reviewed with conclusions drawn. That means that future plans are seen as learning opportunities as opposed to just merely things to be done.

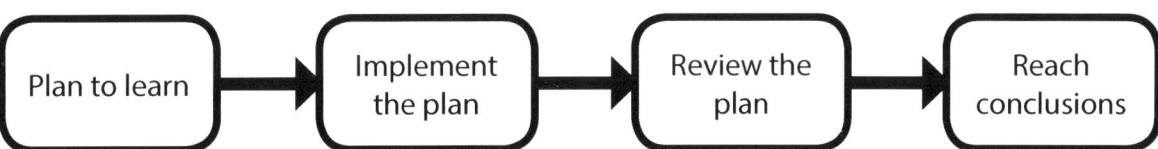

In practice learning, students need to adopt a prospective approach to learning. Students are expected to identify their learning needs, to participate in the development of a curriculum, to engage in the available learning opportunities, to keep their learning under review and to reach conclusions about their learning. Where students have a tendency to follow one of the other approaches, you may need to work with them to help them develop the prospective approach.

Surface and Deep Approaches to Learning

First identified in 1976 by Marton and Saljo, most people involved in adult learning have heard of the terms deep learning and surface learning as this is a widely used concept in adult learning.

- *Surface approach*
  This approach focuses on acquiring and memorising information. An uncritical, unquestioning approach is taken to acquiring new knowledge and there is little reflection. Learning is motivated by external factors such as demands from employers or assessment requirements.

- *Deep approach*
  This approach involves critically analysing new ideas and linking them with existing knowledge. This approach means that a student will understand and be able to apply the learning in new and different contexts. Deep learning assists with problem solving and making wider connections.

It is important to note that these approaches are not based on personality types, but can be adopted.

"We should not identify the student with a fixed approach to learning,…. It is the design of learning opportunity that encourages students to adopt a particular approach… Very crudely: deep is good, surface is bad and we should teach in a way that encourages students to adopt a deep approach."

(Houghton 2004:2)

Thinking Styles

Danbury (1994) identified that people have two different thinking styles:

- Pictorial
- Verbal

Pictorial Thinkers

Pictorial thinkers have pictorial memories. They think visually. They are attracted to visual images, they like flowcharts, diagrams, ecomaps. Pictorial thinkers often learn and remember issues drawing on visual imagery.

Verbal Thinkers

Verbal thinkers have verbal memories. They think in words rather than pictures. Verbal thinkers will learn best through reading and discussion. Diagrams and imagery will have little meaning for them.

It's worth asking a student which style they think they have and adapting the methods you use to suit their style.

IN SUMMARY

This brief and basic review of theories of adult learning should have helped to develop your understanding of how adults learn and this information should help you to deliver effective practice learning opportunities for students. Most of what has been covered is summed up well in the following statement: first made by Confucius back in 450BC.

"Tell me and I will forget, show me and I might remember, involve me and I will understand".

12 CRITICAL REFLECTION AND LEARNING

Experiential learning illustrates the importance of learners reflecting on their experiences in order to learn. Reflective practice is a vital aspect of social work and the word reflection regularly comes up in terms of social work practice learning. It is therefore vital that those involved in practice learning have at least a basic idea of the process of reflection and specifically how it can aid learning and development.

Schön (1987) asserted that there are two types of reflection:

- Reflection IN action
- Reflection ON action

In 1991 Killian and Todnem extended Schön's ideas by proposing third type of reflection:

- Reflection FOR action

Essentially, these forms of reflection can be summarised as:

Reflection for action	Reflecting in preparation for an event
Reflection in action	Reflecting as an event is occurring
Reflection on action	Reflecting after an event has occurred

Effectively, this creates a reflective cycle:

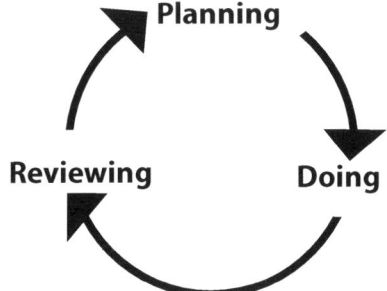

Reflection for Action

This is the reflecting you do in preparation for an event. It involves planning for practice and anticipating what you might do considering a range of possibilities and outcomes. Based on my own practice and on talking to both students and practitioners, I feel that there is a tendency to reflect for action more when you are asked to carry out something unfamiliar. It is likely therefore that students will need additional time to reflect for action - that is to think through what 'might' happen and how they might deal with it. Reflection for action is based on anticipation, rather than fact or evidence and so is limited in terms of outcomes.

Reflection in Action

Reflection in action is the process of reflection when you are engaging in an activity. Essentially it is working and being aware of what you are doing at the same time. Reflection in action involves:

- Thinking ahead (Right if that's happened, then I need to .....")
- Being critical ("That didn't work very well....")
- Storing up experiences for the future ("I could have dealt with that better, next time I will try....")
- Analysing what is happening ("She's saying that to test me – I think I should....")

Reflection in action is happening all the time – if your mind is on the task! We all know people who are planning their night out whilst carrying out a task and would all agree that this doesn't constitute good practice. Having your mind on the job is important. Not only is it good practice but it constitutes reflection in action.

Whilst reflection in action is good practice and can help people to develop their practice, it does have drawbacks. The main problems with reflection in action are:

- You can only see things from your own perspective ("I think, I feel, I'm not sure....")
- You will only have short term reflection. If your mind is on the task at hand, when the task changes so will your thoughts.

Reflection on Action

This is the reflecting you do after an event. Reflection on action refers to the process of thinking through and perhaps discussing the incident with a colleague or a supervisor.

Reflection on action is free from urgency and any pressures of the actual event. As such it allows for longer term reflection. You can also ensure that by seeking feedback you use other people's perspectives in your reflection.

The main drawback of reflection on action is that because of time constraints we tend only to think in this way about more complex or critical work issues. Therefore in terms of more routine events and work practice, we tend only to "reflect in action". This can lead us to not making much improvement in our routine work practice. It is important therefore to plan reflection on action to ensure that it covers every aspect of practice.

Improving Practice

Reflective practice supports learning in a range of ways. Perhaps most importantly, reflective practice opens up options; when we reflect on a situation, it enables us both to see more and to see things differently. Effectively, it 'illuminates our practice' so that we can see things more clearly. This can lead to more creative practice, which is important in the current climate and seemingly ever decreasing resources. Brown and Rutter (2006:41) claim that:

Reflecting... helps you to deliver good practice, as you become more able to develop and articulate the resources and services for your service users and be accountable for them.

Bolton (2001) asserts that reflective practice improves practice as it:

- Helps practitioners to identify gaps in their skills and knowledge
- This makes it easier for them to identify their learning needs and improve their practice
- Encourages practitioners to analyse communication and relationships. This means that relationships can be improved and therefore collaborative working is improved too
- Supports practitioners in examining the decision-making process, which can help them to justify practice
- Encourages a healthy questioning approach which can help practitioners to 'find their way'

Knowledge, skills and values

Effective social work practice is made up of knowledge, skills and values, as recognised in the PCF. Critical reflection can improve practice in relation to knowledge, skills and values:

- Reflection can help practitioners to identify gaps in and extend their knowledge. It can also assist in making links so that people can develop ideas about how to use their existing knowledge in new situations
- Reflection can help aid skill development; when you reflect on how you handle a situation and think about the feedback you have had, it can help to develop skills further
- Reflecting on values can help practitioners to be more aware of their values and can assist in dealing with value conflicts

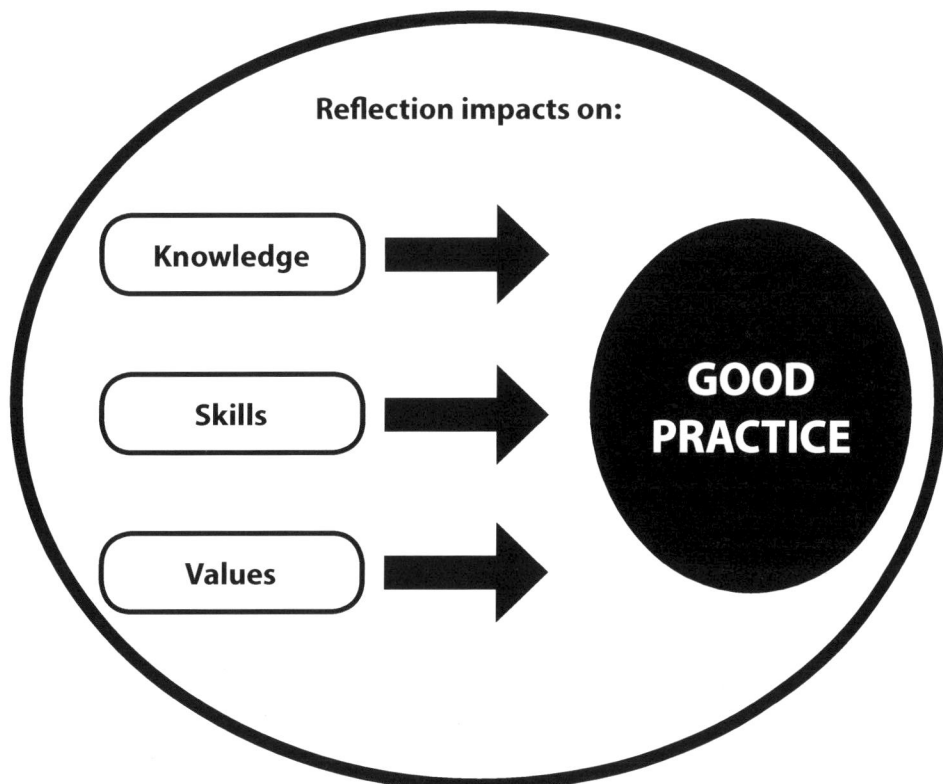

Supporting reflective learning

Practice educators and placement supervisors can assist students to learn more effectively by modelling reflective practice techniques and by encouraging the student to reflect on their experiences. Supervision can provide a safe environment to support students to reflect for and on action.

Two key concepts can help in providing a reflective learning environment:

Critical friendships

The concept of critical friendships was first introduced by Stenhouse (1975) as a method to support action research. The concept has more recently been developed as something which supports reflective practice. The idea of this is that the critical friend acts as an interested 'sounding board'. The critical friend listens to the practitioner and asks pro-active questions which promote deeper thinking and encourage the practitioner to reflect on their work.

Research into the use of critical friends in medical education indicates that whilst having a critical friend is useful, it might be even more advantageous for the person acting as the critical friend in terms of the development of reflective practice skills (Dahlgren et al 2006).

Practice educators and placement supervisors should act as a critical friend to a student, both within supervision and informally in the placement setting.

Dynamic questioning

Reflective practice is fundamentally about exploration and inquiry. As such, asking probing questions can assist people to develop and deepen their reflection. It is important to recognise, however, that encouraging reflection is not just about asking a question, finding an answer and moving on. In fact it requires a dynamic approach to questions which means:

- ✓ there is more than one answer to a question
- ✓ each question can raise another question
- ✓ questions prompt significant changes in the way a person looks at a situation

McClure (2002: 5-6) provides a range of 'reflective questions' which can be adapted as follows for use with a student:

- What were you aiming for when you did...?
- What exactly did you do?
- What theories / models / research informed your practice?
- What were you trying to achieve?
- What did you do next?
- What were the reasons for doing that?

- How successful was it?
- What criteria are you using to judge success?
- What alternatives were there?
- Could you have dealt with the situation better?
- How could you do it differently next time?
- How do you feel about the whole experience?
- How did the service user feel about it?
- How do you know they felt like that?
- What sense can you make of this in light of your past experiences?

We find that using GEMS questions drawn from solution focussed approaches (de Shazer 1985) can also be useful in prompting reflective learning:

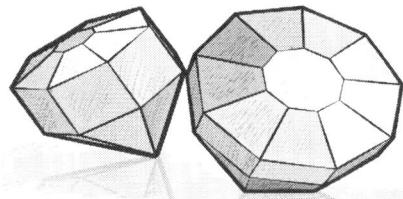

G - Goal setting questions
E - Exception finding questions
M - Miracle questions
S - Scaling questions

Goal setting questions: Goal setting questions are designed to assist the student to identify the goals for their intervention Goal setting questions might encourage the student to think about their goals or those of the service user. Examples include:

- What is the service user hoping to get out of your intervention?
- What are you hoping to achieve?
- How will you know when your goals have been achieved?
- What outcomes are you looking for?

Exception finding questions: These are questions that support the student to identify the successful strategies they have used in the past. The intention is to help the student to move away from a problem focussed narrative to a recognition of their capabilities. These questions will support the student to see what resources and strengths they have and will give them the confidence to apply their own strategies to resolve what they see as impossible situations. Examples include:

- You say you've no idea what to do. When you've faced 'no solution' situations before, what have you done?
- We've discovered that you're skilled at developing intervention plans. How might you draw on these skills now?

Miracle questions: Widely used in social work practice, miracle questions can help students think about how their intervention and practice could be different. The most common miracle questions like *"If you had a magic wand, what would you do with it?"* or *"if you had three wishes to use on this case, what would they be?"* could be useful to help the student look differently at the situation, although they are likely to

simply lead to responses about the need for more resources or easier access to services. More creative miracle questioning can really prompt deeper thinking and more creative practice. For example,

- If you had a time machine and could go back to any stage of this person's life, at what point would you have intervened? Why?
- If you could design a machine to do everything that would be needed in this situation, what would it look like and what would it do?

Scaling questions: Scaling questions are often used in risk assessment and in assessing eligibility for services etc. Scaling questions can be helpful in a range of ways in working with students, for example, in developing a confidence checklist (see page 69). In developing deeper reflection about learning experiences, it can be useful to ask a student questions like:

- On a scale of 1 to 10, how responsible do you feel for what happened?
- You said you're unsure about that. On a scale of 1 to 10, how confident are you?

Within supervision, it can be particularly useful to think about following up scaling questions with 'tailed' questions, such as "You say you are on a 4: What would it take to make you feel more like 8 or 9?"

Supporting the development of reflective practice

Biggs (1999: 6) says that "a reflection in a mirror is an exact replica of what is in front of it. Reflection in professional practice, however, gives back not what it *is* but what it *might be*, an improvement on the original." A good practice educator will effectively hold up a mirror for a student, so that they can "see" their practice clearly. They will also help the student to consider how their practice could look as they develop their skills and knowledge further and improve their practice.

IN SOCIAL WORK
REFLECTIVE PRACTICE THROWS UP MANY POSSIBILITIES

IN SUMMARY

Reflective practice is an important aspect of social work practice and it is therefore important to encourage students towards becoming a reflective practitioner. Taking a reflective approach is vital in enhancing learning and development and therefore practice educators and placement supervisors need to use reflective techniques in facilitating learning.

13 SETTING THE LEARNING AGENDA

As part of the preparation for practice learning, practice educators need to work in partnership with students to set the agenda for learning. It's common practice to ask students about their learning needs. However, "what are your learning needs?" is a potentially difficult question to answer when you don't know what you don't know! As practice educators, we have designed a range of activities which can help students to identify their learning needs and set the agenda for learning.

Bring and Buy

A very straightforward activity – this involves the student working on a list of what they are bringing to the placement. This might include experiences, skills, knowledge and personal characteristics. The student also devises a list of what they want to "buy" – ie: what do they want to get from the placement? Students generally find this question much easier to answer than "What are your learning needs?"

Bring	Buy

This exercise has a number of strengths:

- It's much easier for students to identify with the exercise rather than a more abstract question about learning needs
- Asking the student to initially identify what they are bringing, values the student's experiences and helps to avoid the "deskilling" which many students feel at the outset of a practice learning process.

Confidence Checklist

An alternative approach to supporting a student to identify their learning needs is to devise a "confidence checklist" for the student to complete.

The idea here is that the practice educator devises a list based on what they feel are key tasks, skills and knowledge in the practice learning environment. Potentially, the list could be endless and the practice educator needs to prioritise key areas. The student then works down the list ticking whether this is an area which they are confident in or not. Alternatively, the student could score each area on a scale of 1 to 10 – 10 being very confident, 1 being very unsure. The student and practice educator can then work together to devise action to support the student as required. The checklist can be returned to in supervision later in the placement. Actions can be reviewed and the student can be asked to re-score themselves in each area. Occasionally students feel less confident as the placement progresses and they realise all that is entailed in each task (as demonstrated in the theory of cognitive dissonance – see pages 58-59). This can lead to interesting discussions about initial thoughts and subsequent experiences.

Example confidence checklist

Issue/Task	Confident	Not Confident	Action required	Achieved
Using an electronic diary				
Meeting new people				
Answering the telephone				
Writing case notes				
Speaking up/ challenging				
Approaching a manager				
Completing a referral form				
Completing an assessment				
Working with other professionals				
Financial calculations				

Using exercises such as these – or one you design yourself, should help identify the student's unique learning needs.

Clearly all students need to learn about the application of the Professional Capabilities Framework (PCF) within the particular practice learning setting.

The unique learning agenda for each practice learning opportunity will therefore be a balance of the PCF and the HCPC Standards of Proficiency matched against the learning needs of the particular student. Once this agenda is clarified, you are ready to begin working on developing a plan for the student's learning. Sometimes referred to as a practice learning plan or a learning curriculum, this is a key document negotiated between the practice educator and student.

Learning Curriculums

The main 'education' role of the practice educator is to ensure, as far as possible, that the learning opportunities offered to the student are matched to their learning needs. This is often done through the devising of a learning curriculum. Whilst developing a written learning curriculum is not essential within most social work programmes, it is considered good practice. Where a written curriculum is devised, a copy should be attached to the practice learning agreement.

Learning curriculums, sometimes known as practice learning plans, are simply what they say they are. They are a written statement of the individual student's learning needs and a plan of how these will be addressed through the practice learning opportunity.

There are many different methods of formulating a learning curriculum and you will need to devise one that is acceptable and accessible to both you and the student. The actual style of the document is not important. However, the curriculum should detail the student's learning needs, the learning methods and materials to be used, the learning opportunities that will be sought and possibly some expected outcomes. Some students will offer learning needs, which seem to be unrelated to the assessment criteria and you may need to negotiate these, or at least prioritise the learning needs that relate to the assessment criteria. With the implementation of the PCF, an increasing number of practice educators are devising a learning curriculum around the nine domains.

The learning curriculum should be reviewed on a regular basis and it may help to give actual dates of review in the document.

There are various advantages to the use of learning curriculums:

- The drafting of a curriculum will lead to some meaningful negotiation with students. The plans you make will therefore have more relevance to the student and you will probably find that they are more committed, due to having some "ownership" of the plans.
- The curriculum will give some focus to the practice learning opportunity. It should also structure the learning process, though clearly there should still be flexibility. This is important since placements can seem very short considering the amount of work there is to do. The use of a learning curriculum and the regular review process, will ensure that nothing is "missed out" or taken over by other issues.
- The use of a learning curriculum will ensure that each student that comes to your placement site has a unique learning experience, tailored to their specific needs.
- The use of a learning curriculum should help to focus the choice of work the student undertakes, ensuring that this meets their learning needs.

Off Site Practice Education and Learning Curriculums

Learning curriculums are particularly useful in off site practice learning situations. They ensure that the practice educator and on site supervisor are each aware of their own particular role in facilitating the student's learning and also enable the student to be totally clear about roles and responsibilities.

The student, practice educator and on site supervisor should meet together, either before the placement begins, or very early in the placement (whichever is agreeable to all parties) and negotiate, in detail, a practice learning plan/curriculum. It is also useful in off site practice learning to make the review of the plan more formal (eg: on exact dates) and to ensure that all parties are once again involved in the review.

Addressing Specific Learning Requirements

It is vital to ensure that any specific learning requirements a student has are clearly addressed in the provision of learning opportunities. Advice is offered on this in Chapter 30. Negotiating a learning curriculum with the student can assist in this – as opportunities are agreed you should ensure the student feels these opportunities they are accessible and address any specific requirements they have.

Ideas for Devising a Learning Curriculum

We have seen and used various styles of curriculums. They all work, so the most important thing is to find a style that suits you and the student.

Some people use a box style similar to the following:

Learning Needs	Opportunities	Responsibility	Review	Outcomes	Notes
Here the learning needs will be detailed one by one. Some simply list the PCF domains here, some put student's individual needs, others write a combination of the two.	Detail is provided here about the specific learning opportunities which will meet each need. See Chapter 14 for information about possible learning opportunities	Who is responsible for ensuring the opportunity is provided, will be detailed here.	A date to review whether the learning need is met will be given.	Some people record what the student might be expected to produce eg: a reflective account. Others record what the student will know or be able to do when the learning has been achieved	It's useful to leave a column to write additional notes - a record can be made of how the student feels about the learning, what other learning needs the learning has identified etc.
Further development of assessment skills	1. Shadowing team members carrying out various forms of assessments. 2. Review of assessment documentation and reading assessment policy/procedures/agency standards 3. Carrying out an assessment with a co-worker 4. Undertake low level need assessments 5. Produce some notes on theories around assessment practice	1. Team colleagues and student 2. Student - practice educator to provide information 3. Student and co-worker 4. Student 5. Student	7.8.09 1.7.09 by 21.8.09 by 31.8.09 14.9.09	1. Student to complete shadowing forms 2. Discussion in supervision: student to demonstrate understanding 3. Completed assessment documentation 4. Completed assessment documentation 5. Notes to be discussed in supervision	Student found shadowing useful: would like additional opportunity to shadow carers assessment worker Student now feels confident to undertake assessments

Others use a spider diagram, containing similar information. For example:

LEARNING NEED: *Development of skills in collaborative working*

- **Opportunity:** *Read Working Together Guidance*
  - Responsibility: *student*
  - Review date
  - Outcome: *improved understanding of requirements*

- **Opportunity:** *Shadowing a range of other professionals*
  - Responsibility: *PE/Supervisor to arrange*
  - Review date
  - Outcome: *developing understanding of different perspectives*

- **Opportunity:** *allocation of case work involving collaborative practice*
  - Responsibility: *supervisor*
  - Review date
  - Outcome: *opportunities to develop skills*

- **Opportunity:** *Critical reflections on experiences*
  - Responsibility: *student*
  - Review date
  - Outcome: *reflection on advantages and challenges of collaborative practice*

Some students find this approach accessible – particularly if they use mind map approaches to taking notes. It can be particularly helpful for students with some forms of dyslexia.

Another style involves simply writing each learning need on a separate page and detailing opportunities, responsibilities etc on that page. For example:

Learning Need: *development of ability to apply theory to practice*

Opportunity	Responsibility
1. reading on theories (specific to context)	PE to recommend student to read
2. supervision discussion	PE and student
3. reflective accounts focussing on use of theories in practice	Student
4. academic work - practice analysis	Student
5. use of specific theory exercise (theory circles)	PE to provide exercise - student to reflect on this

Outcomes
Student to feel more confident about the use of theory in social work practice.

Notes
Reviewed at mid point - student would like more opportunity to explore use of theory in practice - specific exercises identified for use in supervision.

The actual style of recording the curriculum isn't important – as long as everyone involved understands it. Whatever style attracts you or whatever style you devise, the most important thing is that the curriculum is a working document which is used and kept under regular review throughout the placement.

IN SUMMARY
Negotiation with the student is key in agreeing the learning agenda for any placement. Empowering the student such that they are able to honestly identify their learning needs and any specific requirements they have will ensure that you can work to effectively facilitate their learning. If this stage isn't adequately addressed, the student may not learn effectively from the experiences provided.

14 LEARNING OPPORTUNITIES

The range of learning opportunities that can be used to facilitate a student's learning is potentially vast as the following diagram (which is not exhaustive) highlights:

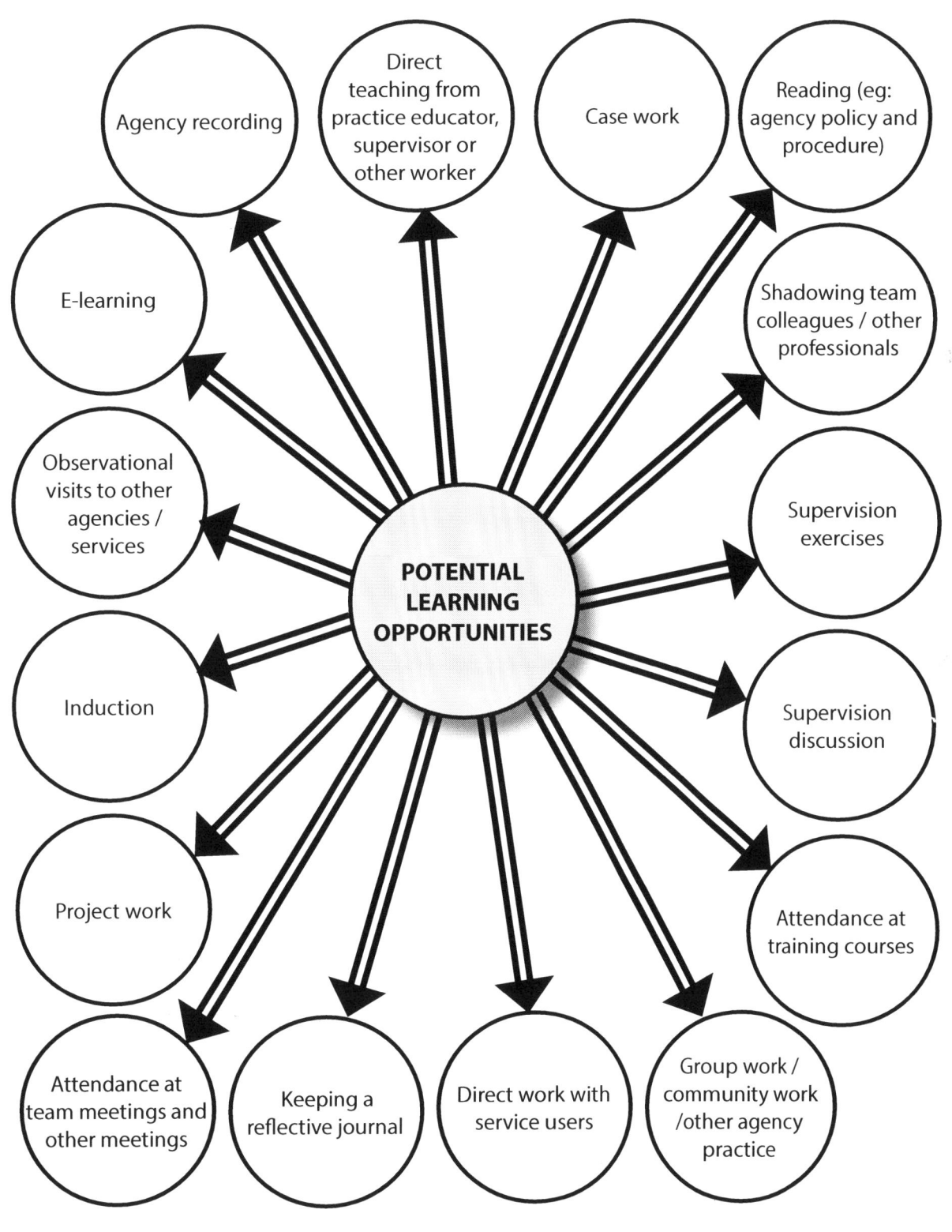

One of the most important things to remember in terms of providing an appropriate range of learning opportunities is that in order to learn from each opportunity, students need the opportunity to reflect and to move around the learning cycle. Simply throwing lots of opportunities at people will not ensure they learn – however good the opportunity is. Returning to Kolb's experiential learning cycle, students will need to:

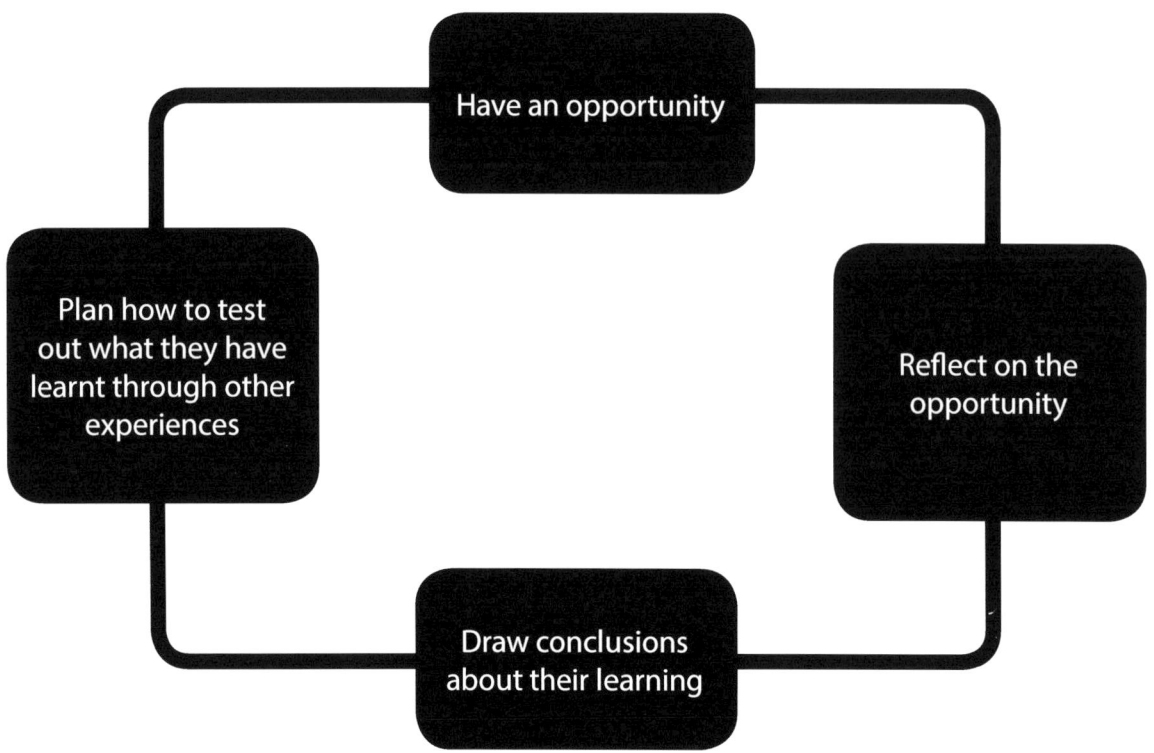

This chapter will work through some of the potential learning opportunities highlighted on the previous page - giving ideas about how students can be assisted to move around the full cycle following the experience.

Induction

There are two components to an induction:

- Induction pack: what the student is provided with at the start of their placement
- Induction programme: what the student does for the first part of their placement

Your agency is likely to have an induction policy and may have a standard induction pack. This can be used as a starting point and must certainly be referred to. However, it is likely that fairly significant changes will need to be made to any standard induction format. For example, some agency induction programmes are designed to spread over up to 12 weeks, which is clearly too long for a student placement – by the time the student has completed induction, there will be little or no time left in the placement. Some agency induction packs contain information on pay systems, pension entitlements etc. – clearly important for employees but not relevant for students. It is essential therefore to review any standard induction packs and programmes to see what aspects are relevant and appropriate for students.

Induction Packs

It is important to think through what students need to be provided with in the early stages of their placement. What you should be looking for is an induction pack, not an induction wheelbarrow. It's easy to think about lots of things which would be useful; it may be more difficult to think about what is essential. Some Universities provide guidance on what should be included in a student induction, if so use this. Whatever you provide in an induction pack, do ask the student to evaluate the pack and towards the end of their placement ask if they think anything else would have been useful. It's never too early to start planning for the next placement! Some of our thoughts on what could be included in a student induction pack follow. Remember that this isn't exhaustive – just some guidance to give you a starting point.

INDUCTION PACK CONTENTS

- **Policies and Procedures**
  You should think about the policies and procedures which are essential for the student to read at the outset of their placement and include these in the pack. Many practice educators and supervisors also include a sheet for the student to sign when they have read the policy. It is also useful to include a list of all the policies and procedures of the agency with an indication of where these are to be found. If an induction pack includes copies of all policies and procedures, it is likely to be huge and to intimidate the student at the outset of their placement.

- **Information about the team**
  A list of names, telephone numbers etc is always useful to a student. The team profile will also be useful.

- **Information about the wider organisation**
  Some kind of indication of the structure of the organisation, how the team fits in etc is always useful.

- **Geographical Area**
  Information about the area covered which might include the places to get lunch, public transport information etc is always useful for a student – particularly if they are new to the area themselves.

- **Information about services/resources**
  It is worth including something about relevant local services, resources and other professionals with links to the team. Some information about what the service does and contact details is useful.

- **Housekeeping Issues**
  Key codes for rooms, information about car parking and issues like tea funds are also useful.

- **Applications**
  Sometimes, students need to apply for ID cards, an email account etc. You will need to provide information on what to do and any necessary application forms.

- **Key Dates**
  Dates which need to go into the student's diary should be provided – for example team meeting dates etc.

- **Stationery and equipment**
  Students will need to be provided with anything which is essential to carry out their role. If a diary is an essential part of the role, this should be provided and returned by the student at the end of placement. Many students do have their own diary and placement providers think that they can use this. However, any diary used is likely to contain confidential information, such as service user's names and addresses. This should remain in the agency at the end of the placement – so a diary should be provided which remains agency property.

- **Induction Programme**
  It is always worth including a copy of the programme of activities which the student will undertake as part of their induction.

Induction Programmes

A good induction programme will help the student to learn some of the essential aspects of agency practice and help to orientate the student to the team, clarifying their role within it. Many practice educators and supervisors think a two week induction period is appropriate. In deciding how long any induction should be, it is important to take account of how long the placement is and the fact that students are often anxious to get "on with the job". It's also worth remembering that since the student is coming to the team as a learner rather than a new worker, activities which are traditionally seen as part of an induction can be spread across the whole placement.

Mullins (2005) states that any induction programme should allow for a staged approach to learning with options for information to be revisited and reviewed. This is vitally important for students in practice learning.

The importance of the induction period for the student cannot be underestimated. It sets the tone for the placement – a student who has a well thought out induction will feel valued and welcomed by the team. The induction should help the student prepare effectively for their placement practice and help them to feel more comfortable about what they are about to do.

However, in the enthusiasm to provide a good induction for a student, it's important to remember all the basic principles of adult learning – involve the student in planning the programme as much as possible, ensure you listen effectively to the student's evaluation of the induction etc.

INDUCTION PROGRAMMES

- **First Day**
  It's important to remember how anxious a student will be on their first day. Make sure there is someone appropriate to meet and greet the student (preferably the practice educator or supervisor). It's often a good idea to ask the student to start a little late on their first day so that the person greeting them can devote their time to this activity. Essential issues need to be covered on this first day – such as orientation to the building, health and safety issues etc.

- **Introductions**
  It is important that the student is introduced to all the relevant people – team members, others in the building etc.

- **Shadowing**
  Students can learn a great deal from shadowing (observing) other team members. More information is provided on shadowing on pages 82-83. As part of the induction programme, it's worth arranging for the student to shadow team colleagues undertaking a range of different activities.

- **Observational Visits**
  It's useful for students to undertake visits to a range of relevant local facilities and services. However, it is also important not to provide the student with a programme of two weeks of visits – the more they are away from the team base, the longer it will take for them to integrate with the team. More information is given on observational visits on pages 80-81.

- **Essential training**
  It is important to ensure that the student has access to any essential training. For example, training on how to use computer systems etc.

- **Reading**
  The student will need time to go through the induction pack and undertake any reading of policies and procedures and other essential reading.

- **Reflection**
  Many enthusiastic practice educators and supervisors produce a busy induction programme for students. It's important to get the balance right – you don't want students sitting about thinking they don't have anything to do but you also need to leave sufficient time for the student to reflect on their activities and learn from them.

- **Time with Supervisor/Practice educator**
  It's also important to leave some space in the induction programme for the student to have supervision and to spend time with the practice educator and/or supervisor to go through essential documentation such as the learning agreement and the learning curriculum.

Reading

Practice educators and supervisors should be able to guide students towards useful reading material – this is likely to include reading agency documentation and policies and procedures. Some of this will take place during induction. However, the student is most likely to learn from reading material when it is specifically relevant to the work they are undertaking - so it is important to prioritise what must be read early in the placement and what can be read later on, as and when it applies to the student's practice.

Reading is quite a passive activity and students will need the opportunity to discuss their reading to develop their learning. Use a range of techniques to follow up the learning – you can provide a 'quiz' for students, ask them to take notes to discuss with you or ask them to highlight the most relevant points. Whatever you do to try to bring the reading to life, always make sure that you discuss the reading and its relationship to practice in supervision. Otherwise students may feel they are being asked to read lots of material for no reason.

Direct Teaching

A didactic approach to teaching is basically about telling people how to do things. There will be a few instances during a placement where a practice educator or supervisor may need to take this approach – for example in informing students about specific processes. However, it is important to remember that the main role is that of a facilitator and not a teacher:

"Practice educators will not always be 'experts' in their field and more traditional didactic/ transmission method of teaching…. will not be the most appropriate way for developing professional capability, as well as not being the most appropriate approach for work based learning."

(Williams and Rutter 2007:93)

Observational Visits

The student is likely to spend some time visiting other service providers or establishments and local resources during their induction. However, it is useful if such visits continue through the whole placement. It is likely that a student will find more meaningful learning in visiting a resource when it is particularly relevant to their practice. For example, if a student visits some day services when they are working with a service user and want to make a referral, they are likely to learn more than if they visit during their induction period when they have nothing to associate their experiences with.

It is useful to ask students to make some notes on their observational visits. We find the following format useful. It can assist the student to reflect on their learning and to develop their observational skills.

Student Comments on Observational Visits

Establishment: ....

Date of Visit: ....

| Type of setting |
| How are referrals made? |
| Positives |
| Negatives |
| Anti-oppressive practice issues |
| Future learning needs |

Signed: .... (Student)

Date: ....

Discussed at supervision session .... Date: ....

Signed: .... (Practice educator)

Shadowing Team Colleagues and / or Other Professionals

Students can learn a great deal from shadowing a range of workers. Subsequent discussions comparing and contrasting how different workers might approach similar tasks in different ways can lead to a great deal of learning and can help a student to develop their own unique style.

However, it's important to ensure a structure is in place for the shadowing – the worker being shadowed needs to know how to maximise the student's learning and the student needs to know what they are looking for.

We find the following guidance on offering shadowing experience (which is given to the worker being shadowed) and shadowing form (completed by the student and the worker shadowed) useful in making the most of shadowing opportunities:

GUIDANCE ON OFFERING SHADOWING EXPERIENCE

Thank you for offering a social work student the opportunity to shadow your practice. As you know, learning from good practice role models is very useful and an essential part of social work practice learning.

"Shadowing" can mean different things to different people. Demonstrating capability as a social work student is the responsibility of the student in consultation with their practice educator. However, there are some implications for you, having offered your service to provide the shadowing opportunity.

You will need to explain the context of the work to the student who is to shadow you. This will enable them to maximise their learning from the experience.

The Professional Capabilities Framework (PCF) illustrates the complex nature of social work and the way that knowledge, skills and values connect and interplay. The student needs to consider the nine domains of the PCF, recognising these as interdependent rather than separate. Therefore the student will want to observe how you use your skills in practice and how these skills are informed by your knowledge and professional values. The student should therefore feel able to ask you a range of questions to build on their understanding of the shadowing experience.

The student will be asked to complete a short form about their experience of shadowing and what they have learnt. There is space on this for you to make any comments. For example, you may have observed the student communicating with the service user and/or others, you may have discussed relevant organisational policies with the student and they may have demonstrated they have a good level of understanding of these etc. All of this feedback will be helpful to the practice educator when they are making an assessment of the student's capability.

SHADOWING REPORT

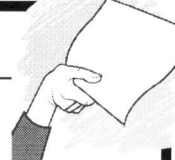

Student's name ....

Name of worker shadowed..

Date of shadowing   ....

STUDENT TO COMPLETE

What did you shadow?

What did you learn from the experience?

What questions do you have as a result of the experience?

Which domains of the Professional Capabilities Framework did you see in action during the shadowing?

What would you like to gain from future shadowing opportunities?

WORKER SHADOWED TO COMPLETE

Comments about the student/shadowing experience

Signed:

.... Student

.... Worker shadowed

Training Courses

Many agencies have a range of in-house training programmes. It may be suitable for students to attend some of these training programmes – especially if they relate to specific areas of their placement practice. However, it is important to remember that students are on placement to experience work – they have formal teaching sessions at University – so attendance on training programmes should be kept to a reasonable level. That said, students do learn a great deal from spending a few days on training programmes – not least from the networking opportunities often linked to these experiences.

Projects

Students can learn a great deal from undertaking project work and teams often benefit significantly from any project work undertaken – a "win win" situation. Essentially, a project should not be an academic piece of work – this is practice learning after all – but outside of this, the range of projects is potentially vast. Examples of some of the projects students we have worked with have undertaken include:

- the development of a resource pack for the team
- development of information packs for service users/carers
- evaluation of outcomes for service users
- development of project plans for specific areas of work with service users
- development of strategies for work with service users whose first language isn't English
- establishing support groups

It's worth asking yourself "what would the team really like to do if we had the time?" as a starting point for ideas – follow this up with "If the student were to undertake this piece of work, would it assist their learning and help them in providing evidence for the against the assessment criteria." If the answer to this is yes, then discuss the potential for the project with the student. Ideas for project work can also come from the student. If a student encounters a problem or sees where an aspect of work could be improved, you could ask the student "what could you do about this?" and a project idea can be generated.

Remember, a student is only with the team for a limited amount of time so any project should be clearly defined and manageable within timescales.

E-learning

E-learning refers to the use of information and communication technologies – such as computer based learning programmes and use of the world wide web (internet) to assist learning. E-learning is widely promoted in all work sectors including social care and social work. As a result, it is likely that students will be used to making use of e-learning tools at University.

Some Universities have set up e-learning programmes which students need to continue to make use of during placement. Some agencies also have e-learning programmes which students can access to assist their learning.

The Social Care Institute for Excellence (SCIE) have a fairly well developed e-learning programme – information can be accessed on their website – www.scie.org.uk.

Some practice educators and supervisors who are not so familiar with technology can be reluctant to advise students to make use of e-learning. However, a great deal can be learnt, by both students and practice educators, from e-learning resources – so it's worth exploring this area.

Reflective Journals

Reflective journals (otherwise known as reflective diaries) can be very useful in supporting students to reflect on their experiences and hence learn from them. Some Universities specifically require students to keep reflective journals during their placement. Many do not make it a set requirement, in which case practice educators might ask students to use reflective journals – either to keep them on an ongoing basis or to write entries on specific experiences. Writing reflective accounts following on from specific experiences can be a great source of learning for students. However, issues about the privacy of the student, the confidentiality of the diary entries and whether the diary will be used as part of the student's assessment all need to be discussed and agreed to maximise the student's learning – if they are focusing more on what the reader might think rather than on their own reflections, the opportunities for learning will be impeded.

> "Some students might benefit from keeping an unstructured reflective journal, as I have. By getting into a regular habit of writing for a few minutes without stopping, I have got a useful record of my own reflections and a way into the more formal writing I am expected to do as a student. The process must, however, be set up properly for students who have never done it before."
> (Sinclair 2006: 23)

Some students know just how they want to write a reflective journal – and it should be a personal choice. However, others look to practice educators and supervisors to provide guidance on how to produce a reflective journal. The Royal Melbourne Institute of Technology University (2007) produce some useful guidance for students around a D-I-E-P formula:

D – Describe objectively what happened – Answer the question "What did I see and hear?"

I – Interpret the events – explain what you saw and heard. (Your new insights; your connections with other learning; your feelings; your hypotheses; your conclusions.) Answer the question "What might it mean?" or "What was the reason I did this activity?"

E – Evaluate the effectiveness of what you observed/learned – make judgements clearly connected to observations made. Evaluation answers the question "What is my opinion about what I observed or experienced? Why?"

P – Plan how this information will be useful to you. What are your recommendations? (Be concrete.) Consider: In what ways might this learning experience serve me in my future?"
(RMIT University 2007)

Students can find it useful to use specific models of reflection as a structure for reflective journals. The Social Work Pocket Guide to Reflective Practice (Maclean 2010) provides guidance on a range of models which students often find useful in developing reflective journals.

Agency Practice

The student should be given the opportunity to engage in a range of agency practice. This might include case work, group work, community work, whatever the practice of the agency! The student will also participate in team meetings and other activities which a worker in the organisation would undertake. However, in ensuring that students have the opportunity to engage in 'real work', it is vital that they are not seen as an extra worker who can be overloaded with work. How work will be allocated to the student must be made clear at the outset of the placement – generally all work for the student should be allocated through the practice educator or supervisor (where relevant). It's not unknown for team members, in their enthusiasm to provide useful opportunities for a student, to overload a student (who doesn't feel able to say no).

It is very difficult to give clear guidance on how much work a student should be expected to undertake – one piece of work could range from minimal to significant. The key is to keep the workload under review with the student to ensure that they feel comfortable with this.

Supervision Exercises and Discussion

Many of the learning opportunities covered in this chapter come together in supervision, certainly the follow up discussion about learning opportunities which will take place in supervision is vitally important. General supervision discussion in itself can be a major learning opportunity for students.

A range of exercises can be given to students for follow up discussion in supervision. For example, Developing a Practice Learning Curriculum (published by ourselves) contains a range of useful exercises and guidance on how to use these in supervision with students. You can of course also devise your own exercises for use in supervision with student – write up a case study for a student, ask them to carry out a specific task or research on a particular area. The potential is endless.

Supervision is such an important aspect of practice learning that the next section is dedicated fully to it.

IN SUMMARY

A vast range of learning opportunities can be made available to students in practice learning. Opportunities should be selected which meet the needs of students and which match their preferred style. It is essential that any specific learning requirements are also considered. The most important thing is that practice educators and supervisors work in partnership with students to select a wide range of opportunities.

15 THE LEARNING ENVIRONMENT

The environment in which adults learn is recognised as vital and you will often hear the term "a safe learning environment." However, since we all have different styles, different needs and individual preferences what one person might consider a safe environment conducive to learning, another might consider as a problematic environment. It is therefore essential, as covered, to discuss the learning environment and what a student might need with them.

To prompt some thoughts about how the learning environment should be organised to create a safe environment and maximise learning, this chapter covers some of the key issues highlighted in relevant literature.

In 1970 Malcolm Knowles introduced the idea of the "learning environment". He asserted that the following issues were important to consider, in relation to the learning environment.

- physical issues
- psychological issues
- social issues
- cultural issues

Knowles argued that if learners' needs in these areas were not met within the environment, their learning would be impeded.

Tisdell (1995) discussed the importance of inclusivity in the learning environment, arguing that a learning environment should:

- *"acknowledge that all individuals bring multiple perspectives as a result of gender, class, age, sexuality etc*

- *recognise that learners' identification with social groups is multiple and complex*

- *reflect the experiences of learners and value these as a basis for learning and assessment*

- *acknowledge the power disparity between teacher and learner"*

(Williams and Rutter 2007:43)

Billington (1996) identifies seven characteristics of effective adult learning environments. Whilst these are about generic learning programmes, we find them very useful in considering the practice learning environment.

The seven key factors she identified were:

1. An environment where students feel safe and supported, where individual needs and uniqueness are honoured, where abilities and life achievements are acknowledged and respected.

2. An environment that fosters intellectual freedom and encourages experimentation and creativity.

3. An environment where students are treated as peers – accepted and respected as intelligent experienced adults whose opinions are listened to, honoured, appreciated.

4. Self directed learning, where students take responsibility for their own learning.

5. Pacing or intellectual challenge. Optimal pacing is challenging people just beyond their present level of ability. If challenged too far beyond, people give up. If challenged too little, they become bored and learn little.

6. Active involvement in learning.

7. Regular feedback mechanisms for students to advise what works best for them and what they want and need to learn – and facilitators who hear and make changes based on student input.

(Billington 1996:2)

Many people who are new to supervising students focus their thoughts about the learning environment on practical and physical characteristics. However, it is important to be aware that the physical environment is only one aspect of the learning environment.

Foord and Haar (2008) claim that work on effective learning environments focuses too significantly on physical and context issues, rather than recognising the importance of relationships and teams. They argue that key aspects to an effective learning environment include:

- relationship-based, collaborative learning opportunities being available
- the opportunity for group reflection
- all workers seeing themselves as learners at different stages

Kejawa (2010) argues that adults are eager to learn when they feel they are in a safe environment. He argues that the most important aspect of a safe learning environment is that it provides space for learners to explore the uncertainty of any skill or theory, providing a safe place for thinking about how their learning is relevant to their context.

IN SUMMARY

Good practice education should create a safe environment for students to learn. Whilst all students are unique and have differing needs and preferences, there are some commonly agreed factors to positive learning environments which practice educators and supervisors should take into account in providing practice learning opportunities.

KEY LEARNING POINTS

- It is helpful to have at least a basic understanding of adult learning theory to assist in facilitating a student's learning.

- The role of a practice educator is about facilitating learning rather than directly teaching

- It is vital to agree the agenda for practice learning by working in partnership with the student

- A well designed learning curriculum will assist in clarifying the learning plan for the student

- A wide range of learning opportunities are available within any practice learning setting

- Reflection enhances learning - both the practice educator and the student need to take a reflective approach to practice learning

- Students should be fully engaged in the learning process and should be assisted to take responsibility for their own learning

- It is important to work to create a safe learning environment in practice learning

- Learning is a two way process – you should take the opportunity to learn as much from your practice education role as possible

SUPERVISING THE STUDENT

One of the major tasks of a practice educator is to provide quality supervision for the student. Supervision is the forum where the majority of the responsibilities of a practice educator come together – for example, supervision will involve discussion about the management of the placement, the student's learning, the progress of assessment etc.

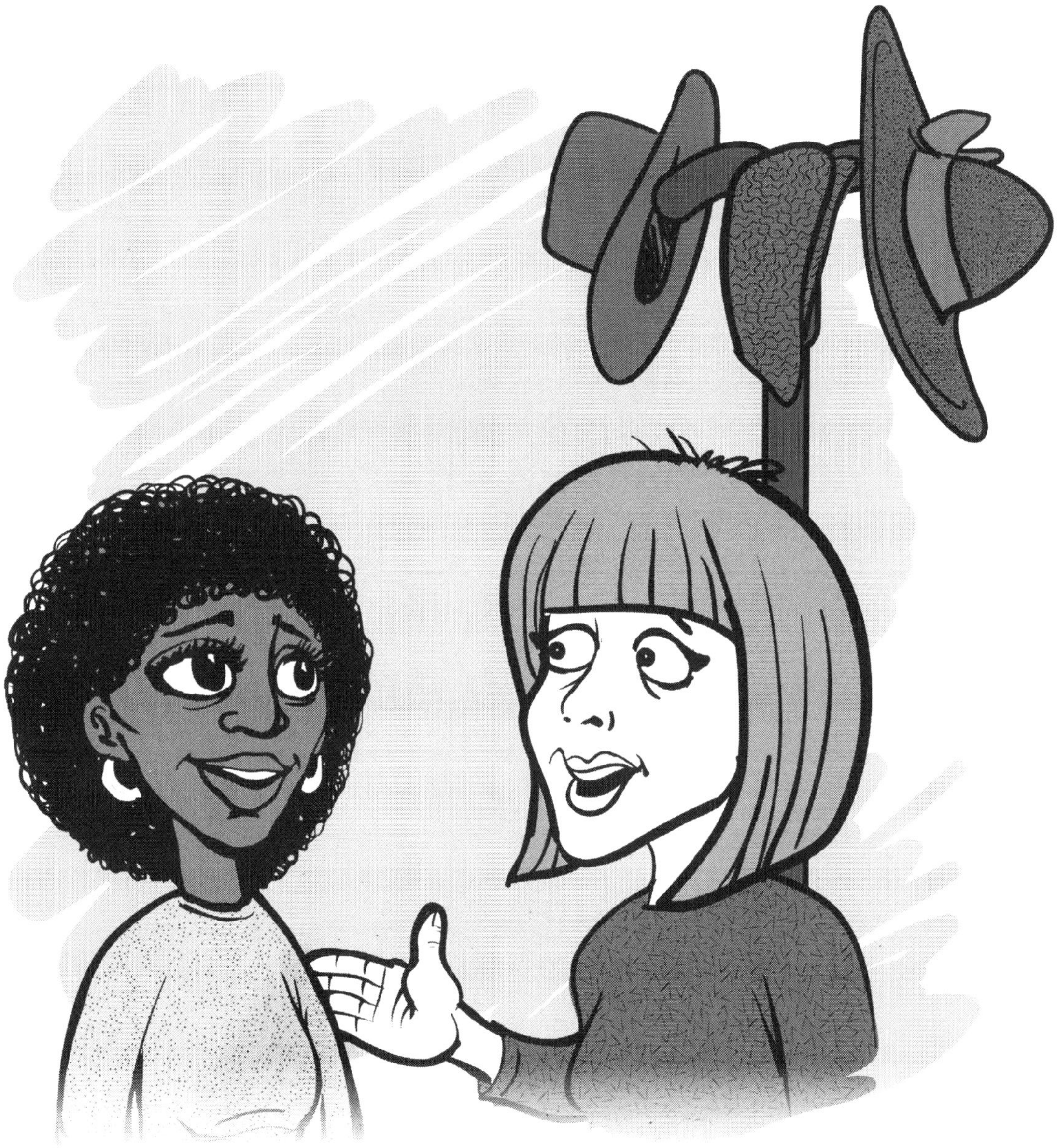

LINKS TO PEPS | DOMAIN B

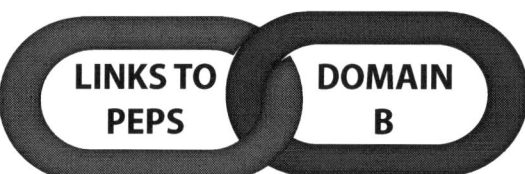

16 AN INTRODUCTION TO STUDENT SUPERVISION

Essentially, supervision forms the "track" on which the practice teaching "train" runs and regular good quality supervision is integral to the success of any practice learning opportunity. The supervisory process becomes a critical part of both enabling and empowering the student to learn and provide evidence of their practice.

Within social work generally, there is often an assumption that because all professionals have received supervision during their career, then they will all be able to provide supervision. Historically, there has been only very limited training on supervision skills, although this is now improving since a number of key Inquiries have pointed out the importance of supervision – for example, the Victoria Climbié Inquiry Report by Lord Laming (2003).

It certainly does not follow that, just because someone has been a supervisee, they will make a good supervisor. Any poor practice within their own supervision experience is likely to be replicated unless they have reflected on their experiences of receiving supervision. It is therefore worthwhile, before taking on a role in providing supervision, to reflect on your own experiences of receiving supervision. What has made supervision a good experience for you? What elements of the supervision you have received have been negative? Reflections such as this can help you to make a checklist of good practice in supervision.

Professional Supervision and Student Supervision

Practice educators and supervisors will not only be giving supervision; they should have supervision of their own. Many are informed by their ongoing experiences of supervision and especially if they have a positive experience, are tempted to replicate this in their provision of supervision to students. However, there are significant differences in the supervision of employed workers (what we term 'professional' supervision) and the supervision of students. Some of the key differences are:

- *Regularity*
  Student supervision will be much more regular than that of workers.

- *Variety of approaches*
  A variety of approaches are likely to be used in student supervision – for example, role play may be employed, case studies used etc. Anything which will facilitate a student's learning may be employed in student supervision. Whilst there may be some variety in supervision with workers, on the whole, professional supervision will focus around discussion about cases.

- *Theory and other underpinning knowledge*
  Whilst student supervision will include discussion about social work theory and other underpinning knowledge, often this is less obvious within professional supervision.

- *Emphasis*
  The emphasis in student supervision is on learning and reflection. Whilst there should be a similar emphasis in professional supervision, this is often not the case. In our experience, the focus of professional supervision is often on accountability for case work.

- *Learning needs*
  Similar to the previous point about the focus of sessions, is the fact that the student's learning needs should be addressed within the supervision process. In fact, the main purpose of student supervision is to address the student's learning needs and ensure that the placement is running smoothly. On the other hand, professional supervision is largely about meeting agency policy in relation to supervision.

- *Assessment*
  Whilst student supervision is all about the student's learning, it is also a forum used for assessing the level of capability achieved by the student. Most professional supervision does not include an assessment element (at least not formally).

- *Direct involvement*
  The person providing supervision to the student (ie: the practice educator and where relevant, the supervisor) will have some direct knowledge of the work the student is doing. They may be co-working cases for example. As a minimum, there will have been a number of direct observations of the student's work. Often the person providing professional supervision has little or no direct knowledge of the work being undertaken – they are reliant on the worker's reports about the work.

- *Recording*
  Since it is likely that the records of student supervision will be used as part of the assessment process, sometimes being included in student portfolios, the recording of student and professional supervision is often significantly different.

- *Length of process/relationship*
  Student supervision relationships are by their very nature short term. When the placement ends, the process and the supervisory relationship also ends. On the other hand, professional supervisory processes and relationships are open ended and usually continue on a long term basis until either the supervisor or supervisee moves positions.

- *Gains/Outcomes*
  It could be argued that because of the assessment aspect, which is intrinsically part of the student supervision process, there is more of an obvious outcome or personal gain for a student than for a worker in supervision.

Perhaps because of the significant differences between the supervision of students and the supervision of workers, there is a long standing significant debate in the practice teaching world about whether we should use the word 'supervision' for what occurs with students. Shardlow and Doel (1996) used the term practice tutorial rather than supervision. Using different terminology can certainly assist students and others involved in practice learning to understand more of what student supervision is about. Some students with no previous professional experiences, for example, are not familiar with the word supervision in the professional context and with the other meanings of the word, this can lead to confusion. However, we would argue that it is both appropriate and useful to use the word supervision. If the same word is used for student supervision and that of workers, it may also lead to a reflection about some of the poor quality of professional supervision and this can only be a good thing. Nevertheless, it is important to recognise the key differences in professional and student supervision.

Having a clear framework for student supervision is important so that everyone is clear about its purpose. We find the following framework for supervision developed and updated by the practice educator support group of Staffordshire Social Care and Health particularly useful in clarifying aspects of supervision. It is meant to provide a framework for discussion between a practice educator and student, but may also form the basis of a supervision agreement between them.

A FRAMEWORK FOR STUDENT SUPERVISION

Definition

Supervision is a structured two-way process, which is used to achieve and maintain professional standards.

Aims

1. Supervision should facilitate students learning, professional and personal development.

2. Supervision should take place on a regular basis. Frequency and duration should be agreed at the outset of the placement.

3. Supervision should be planned, reflective and challenging.

4. An environment should be created which is conducive to learning, where issues of theory and practice can be constructively appraised and challenged.

5. Supervision should address power structures within the practice educator/student relationship and the workplace more generally. Whilst acknowledging the authority of the practice educator in terms of assessment, an equitable atmosphere needs to be achieved.

6. Supervision should focus upon the student's use of self within practice in relation to the boundaries, expectations and policies of the agency.

7. Conflict resolution should take place, in the first instance, within the supervision process. If issues remain unresolved, identified procedures should be followed without delay.

Method

1. Both parties need to give commitment to the process of supervision.

2. Anti-oppressive practice will have a high profile within supervision.

3. The supervision process will comprise of several components, including:
   - Formal teaching
   - Planning and evaluating practice skills
   - Caseload management and accountability
   - Appraising and developing practice
   - Putting theory into practice
   - Evaluating theory in the light of practice
   - Exploring potential learning opportunities as an ongoing process
   - Reviewing learning needs
   - Identifying optimum learning and teaching styles
   - Identifying personal support needs
   - Reviewing the supervision process

4. Formal structured supervision sessions can be complimented by:
   - Informal supervision
   - Peer supervision
   - Group supervision

   All of which can be valuable experiences for students. However, these should be in addition to, rather than instead of, formal two-way sessions. These must also have adequate recordings.

5. Wherever possible, structural and societal imbalances should be made explicit and discussed within supervision.

6. Supervision arrangements will be incorporated in the practice learning agreement. A separate supervision agreement can be drawn up. This ensures that both student and practice educator are aware of the expectations for supervision

7. Supervision, as a process, will be continually evaluated and open to adaptation to meet changing needs.

8. Feedback will be two-way, constructive, balanced and relevant.

9. Supervision agendas should be jointly constructed, with the previously stated aims in mind. Standing items (such as anti-oppressive practice and theory to practice) can be useful to ensure aims are achieved.

10. The boundaries of confidentiality within supervision should be explicitly agreed between the practice educator and student.

(Staffordshire Directorate of Social Care and Health 2005)

IN SUMMARY

Supervision is a core element of practice learning. It is important to be aware of the differences between the supervision of staff and the supervision of students and to have a clear framework for student supervision.

17 FUNCTIONS OF SUPERVISION

Morrison (2005) provides a clear definition of supervision which outlines the commonly agreed four functions of supervision:

"Supervision is a process by which one worker is given responsibility by the organisation to work with another worker(s) in order to meet certain organisational, professional and personal objectives which together promote the best outcomes for service users. These objectives or functions are:

1. *Competent, accountable performance/practice (managerial or normative function)*

2. *Continuing professional development (developmental / formative function)*

3. *Personal support (supportive / restorative function)*

4. *Engaging the individual with the organisation (mediation function)"*

(Morrison 2005:32)

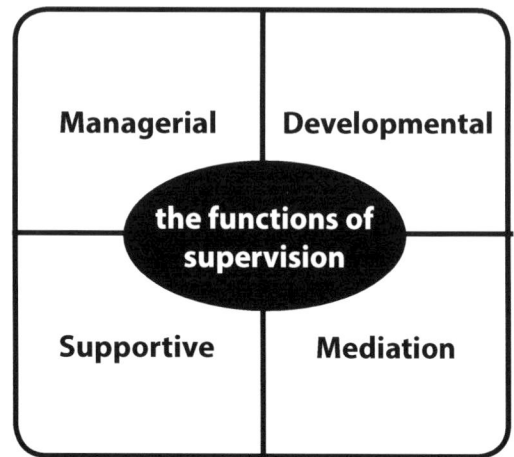

These functions of supervision are commonly reflected in agency supervision policies. They are acknowledged as the key functions of all professional supervision. In our experience, the supervision of qualified staff often focuses on the accountability function at the expense of others. It is essential that in student supervision, all four functions are addressed – with perhaps the primary focus being on the developmental function.

Accountability

A key aspect of any form of supervision is that the supervisee is accountable to the supervisor for their work with service users. In the case of off site arrangements, the on site supervisor is accountable for the student's work – hence the need for students to have supervision sessions with on site supervisors with particular regard to their ongoing work.

Students need to be given the opportunity to discuss their workload, the reason for allocation, the work being carried out, planned or expected outcomes, challenges and concerns. All of these discussions are part of the accountability aspect of supervision – described by Morrison (2005) as the managerial or normative function.

Agencies may have requirements about the recording of case discussion in supervision – for example, a note may need to go on a service user's file when the case has been discussed in supervision. This will need to be considered in the recording of supervision (see Chapter 19).

As stated, it is our experience that some supervision for social workers focuses almost entirely on this function – a review of casework and tasks to be carried out, with perhaps a cursory nod towards other aspects of supervision. Indeed, many practice educators tell us that this is their own experience of receiving supervision. It is vital that this is not replicated with students. That's not to say that practice educators and supervisors should not ask students about their ongoing work with service users – indeed many of the other functions of supervision are addressed by a practice educator's skills in questioning when cases are being discussed.

Professional Development

What Morrison (2005) refers to as the developmental or formative function others (eg: Kadushin 1976) call the educative function. Many poorly skilled supervisors think they have covered this with the question "is there any training you want to go on?" Whilst discussions about training and other learning opportunities is an aspect of this function of supervision, it's about much more than this!

Skilled use of the coaching conversation (see page 56) is very important here. When discussing the work that the student has been doing it's important to ask "and what did you learn from that?" along with a range of other questions designed to encourage the student's reflection. Ensure that supervision is seen as a key element in the student's learning experience. Supervision should provide an opportunity for bringing together learning experiences in a way which allows the student space and time to discuss their thoughts, observations, concerns and difficulties.

In order to create a truly effective learning environment within supervision, it's important to clarify the boundaries of the session, to promote trust and to support the student to feel safe. Good practice in supervision will promote such an environment.

Personal Support

Supervision should be a supportive process. The work which we engage in creates a range of emotions and reactions and students in particular will need support with this. Discussions with some less experienced students highlights the fact that they are being asked to deal with experiences and aspects of deprivation which they didn't even know existed prior to their practice learning experiences. Coupled with this, students are managing not only their workload, but also their learning and any academic requirements. In addition, many students work part time to support themselves financially. Little wonder then that placements can be a very stressful experience for students.

We find that opening a supervision session with a basic question like "how are you feeling this week?" helps to set an appropriate tone for supervision and shows an interest. It's also important to ask a student how they feel about the issues and situations discussed throughout the session. However, it is important to acknowledge boundaries here – a supervision session should not become a counselling session. Supportive supervision is important, but this should not be at the expense of the other functions of supervision. It's not unknown for a student to try to engage a practice educator in discussions about feelings and support to avoid other questions and discussions. Where a student needs support over and above what can be offered within a well balanced supervision session, they should be advised about other support options – most Universities have counselling or welfare services, which may be appropriate.

Whilst it is vitally important to address the supportive function ensure you maintain a balance – you are the student's practice educator not counsellor; this is a learning relationship – the student should not take on a 'client' role.

Mediation

This is the function of supervision less commonly written about. For example, although Morrison (2005) clearly identifies this as a key function, we have found that most agencies have supervision policies which refer to the first three functions, but not mediation. In our view, mediation is a key aspect of all professional supervision but perhaps more so with student supervision.

Morrison (2005:46) asserts that the mediation function of supervision is about:

- negotiating and clarifying team roles and responsibilities
- briefing management about resource deficits or implications
- allocating resources in the most efficient way
- representing supervisees needs to higher management
- consulting and briefing staff about organisational developments or information
- mediating or advocating between workers, within the team, or other parts of the agency or outside agencies

We have found that sometimes students have what could be described as "idealistic" views of social work and what can be achieved. A number of studies (eg: Maclean 2007) have indicated that students are poorly prepared for the current climate of resource scarcity. The mediation function becomes important here in helping students to understand resource issues, agency policy, eligibility for services etc.

As stated, these functions of supervision are generally accepted as the main functions of all supervision with social work and social care. Talking specifically about the supervision of students, Shardlow and Doel (1996) outline the four main functions as:

- Educative – providing an opportunity for students and practice educators to work together to plan work and assess evidence.
- Pastoral – an opportunity to provide the student with personal support in relation to issues which might impact on learning.
- Managerial – an opportunity to ensure that service users receive an acceptable service.
- Administrative – an opportunity to ensure that all administrative and practical arrangements are working well.

Getting the balance between the functions of supervision is important

According to Doel and Shardlow, good supervision balances these functions to ensure that the needs of the student, practice educator and wider organisation are met.

IN SUMMARY

Supervision is generally agreed to have a number of functions. Professional supervision often focuses on the managerial or accountability function at the expense of the others. Student supervision should balance all the functions with a primary focus on the educative/developmental function.

18 FORMS OF SUPERVISION

You will have heard of a variety of different types of supervision. This chapter explores some of the different forms or types of supervision used in social work practice learning.

Direct or Indirect?

Supervision can be described as either direct or indirect. Direct supervision refers to supervision "on the job" – basically discussion, advice and guidance whilst a worker is actually undertaking a task. Whilst direct supervision is regularly used in social care environments where staff are provided with 'on the job' advice and support, it is less common in social work, although it's use is not unknown in some forms of work. Most of the supervision we are used to in social work would be categorised as "indirect" – away from the actual work with specific time set aside for supervision and reflection. Whilst you may engage in some direct supervision with students, it is vital that they have indirect supervision on a regular basis to allow time away from the 'job' and time for reflection. Therefore, all of what we refer to in this guide is indirect supervision.

Informal or Formal?

Informal supervision is unplanned. Basically, any discussion providing advice, guidance and answers to a supervisee's questions is informal supervision. Formal supervision on the other hand, is planned and structured, has a formal agenda and should take place in a private environment with no interruptions. All social work students will need some informal supervision. At the outset of the placement, the student is likely to have lots of questions and will need lots of informal supervision but this need should decrease over time. One of the characteristics of informal supervision is that it isn't recorded. Since students will need lots of informal supervision, we would advise some recording is kept on this - see pages 136-137 for advice on rolling records. It is likely in off site practice learning arrangements that this informal supervision will be provided by the on site supervisor.

Informal supervision, however regular, cannot replace formal supervision in practice learning. Students must receive regular formal supervision.

Group or Individual

Group supervision is growing in popularity in practice learning. Indeed, some programmes have specifically developed group practice learning models with great success. For more information on this, see Sue Atherton's book "Putting Group Learning into Practice in Social Work Education" (2006).

However, general practice involves students having individual supervision with their practice educator (ie: two way). Whilst occasional group supervision can be really helpful for students, a whole placement group supervision approach should not be used without agreement from the University.

Using the three subheadings above, it is clear that all supervision can be categorised as either:

- Direct or indirect
- Formal or informal
- Group or individual

All students should receive regular indirect, formal, individual supervision, but this can be supplemented by other forms of supervision to enhance the student's learning.

Agency Practice

Some agencies have additional supervision arrangements. For example, some have peer supervision sessions (where groups of individuals working in similar roles consult about their work) or clinical supervision (specific professional supervision provided by someone other than the supervisee's line manager).

Students can participate in these arrangements in order to develop and extend their learning. However, it is vital that this supplements, rather than replaces, formal supervision between the student and practice educator.

IN SUMMARY

There are various forms of supervision. Students can benefit from experiencing all of these. However, students must have regular formal supervision sessions with their practice educator.

19 PRACTICALITIES OF STUDENT SUPERVISION

So far, this section has looked at aspects of good practice in supervision. Some practical issues about the provision of student supervision remain. This chapter will consider some of these practicalities.

Supervision Agreements

It is vital to have a clear agreement about supervision which details issues such as the regularity, venue, agenda, duration, boundaries and responsibilities. Some practice educators devote a section of the learning agreement to this; others devise a separate supervision agreement. If you plan to use your standard agency agreement, you need to be aware of the key differences in student supervision and the supervision of staff, as covered in Chapter 16 and to amend the supervision agreement accordingly.

Frequency and Duration

Students should have regular formal supervision sessions with their practice educator. Most programmes have their own requirements on frequency and duration – check out the programme handbook. To give an idea, a common requirement is that students spend two hours a week in formal supervision – for part time students, this would be provided on a pro rata basis. In addition to these formal sessions, the student should be able to access informal consultation at other times (in the case of off site practice teaching, this informal consultation will be provided by the on site supervisor).

Venue and other Practical Arrangements

Supervision should always take place in a private venue where there will be no interruptions. Part of the preparation for practice learning will be identifying a suitable room for supervision. The actual environment isn't that important – it's rare for social work practice learning environments to have beautifully decorated rooms with plush comfortable furniture. It is, however, worth considering some of the practical issues of the environment, as this can be so intrinsically linked to power. For example, if there is a desk or table, can you both sit on the same side? If there are only two chairs and one is substantially higher or bigger than the other, can the student take this one? Basically, all the aspects of environmental issues and power which you will be aware of from your work should be considered in relation to supervision venue arrangements. Don't forget some of the basics too – like switching off phones in the room and putting a note on the door to avoid any interruptions.

Recording Supervision

It is vital that supervision is accurately recorded. It is the practice educator's responsibility to ensure that supervision is accurately recorded – but that does not mean that the practice educator has to do all of the actual recording. This can be negotiated. It is common practice for practice educators and students to take turns in recording sessions, whilst some practice educators expect the student to record all the sessions and others do all the recording themselves.

Some programmes provide their own pro forma for supervision notes and others offer guidance on how they expect sessions to be recorded – always check the programme handbook. Where programmes do not provide a pro forma, practice educators can negotiate with the student, the exact nature of the recording. We find the following format useful:

SUPERVISION NOTES

Student: ....

Practice Educator: ....

Others present: ....

Date: .... Session No: ....

Session No: ....

Agenda

Issue	Notes of discussion	Action

Signed and agreed by:

Practice Educator: ....

Student: ....

Date of next session: ....

It's important that whatever format is used, the notes are sufficiently comprehensive to provide a clear record of:

- the student's experiences
- learning gained
- progress
- advice and guidance given to the student
- any disagreements, concerns, complaints etc.

The notes should also be comprehensible to third parties – some programmes require supervision notes to be included in the student's portfolio as a central piece of evidence. This means that the notes will be read by others at various stages of the assessment process.

Records of supervision should always be agreed by both the student and the practice educator and they should be signed by both parties to demonstrate that they have been shared. In the case of any disagreements about the recording, this should be recorded in the notes. Both parties can make a separate record of their different perspectives with both sets shared and signed to indicate that they have been shared.

Whether notes are handwritten or typed is generally open to negotiation – although some programmes/agencies have expectations that notes are typed. The format of recording must be discussed and agreed with the student and where students have specific needs, these must be addressed in the format of the recording. For example, some students with dyslexia find certain fonts more accessible and some find coloured paper assists in access. Students with a visual impairment may prefer audio notes or a large font format.

Another aspect to consider in terms of recording is what is recorded about service users. Many agencies expect a record to be kept on a service user's file about discussion in supervision. This is good practice, as it helps workers new to a case to familiarise themselves with what has been discussed and what key decisions have been based on; it also enables a service user, who accesses their records, to see what role supervision has played. However, if student supervision notes go in their portfolio, it is important to consider issues of confidentiality in terms of what is included about service users. Our own practice involves never recording service users' names on student supervision records – all service users are identified through the use of an alphabetical code – A, B, C etc. Separate, brief record is made in the service user's file to meet agency requirements on accountability. Check your agency policy and talk to other practice educators in your agency about how they manage this dilemma.

The method of recording should also be considered. Some practice educators make brief contemporaneous notes and complete the full record following the session. Others type the notes straight onto the computer during the session. There are advantages and disadvantages to any method used – but in any case, the method of recording should be discussed with the student to ensure they are comfortable with it. Some students find a supervision session where the practice educator is producing notes on a computer depersonalising and lacking in eye contact.

IN SUMMARY

Practice educators and supervisors will develop their own unique style of supervision within the overall boundaries of good practice. There are however, a number of key practical issues to be considered in providing student supervision.

KEY LEARNING POINTS

- Supervision is a vital forum for both facilitating the student's learning and assessing the student's capability

- Supervision has a number of functions. These should all be balanced to ensure good quality supervision and positive experiences

- Supervision can take a number of forms but students all need to receive formal supervision with their practice educator

- Supervision records are a vital document in practice learning

- The practicalities of supervision should be considered by practice educators and agreed with students

ASSESSING THE STUDENT

An essential aspect of the practice educator role is to assess whether the student has developed professional capability in the practice learning environment. This section explores holistic assessment, the process of assessment, the common sources of error in assessment and how to complete the assessment of the student.

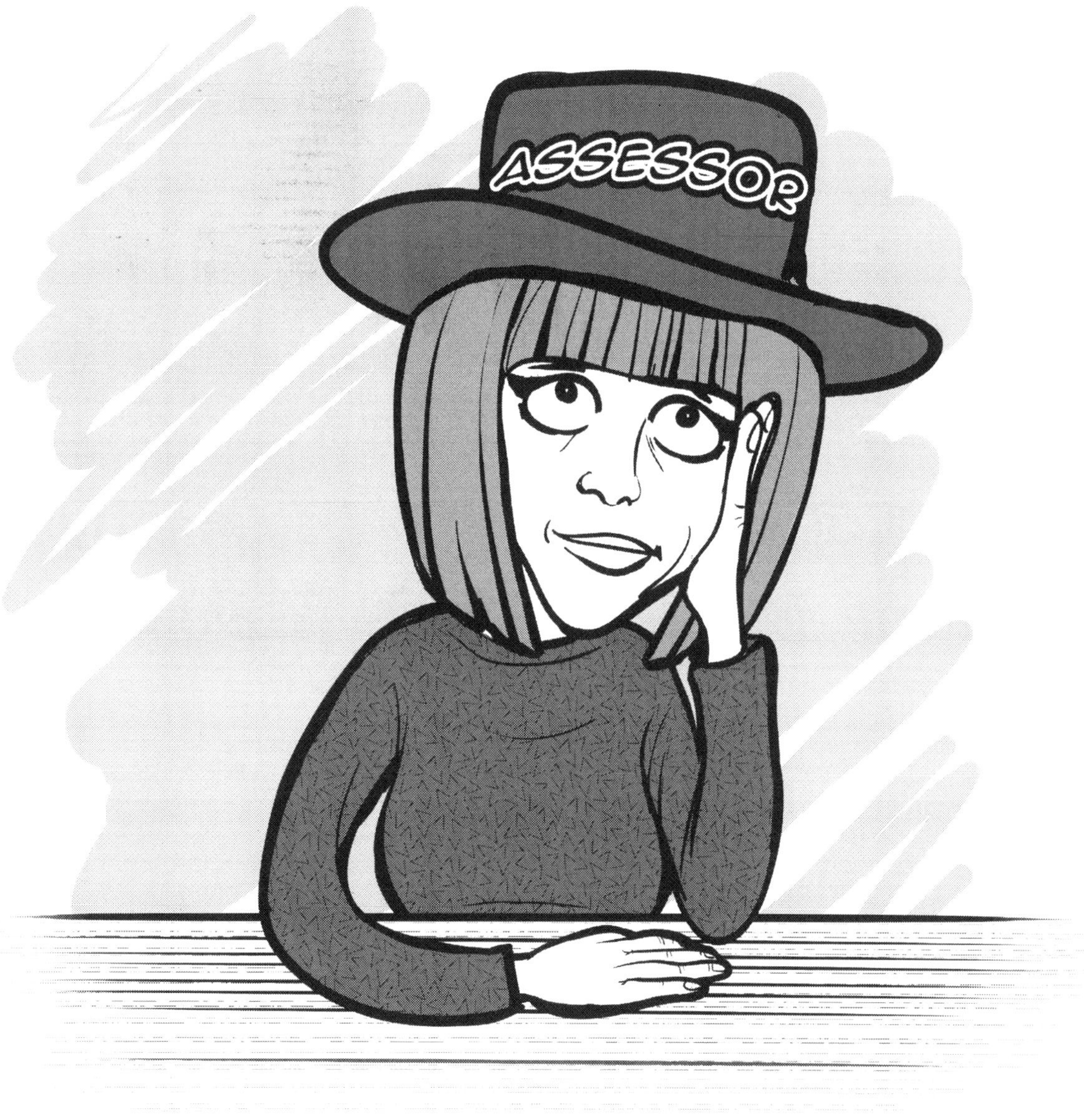

20 THE CONTEMPORARY FRAMEWORK FOR ASSESSMENT IN PRACTICE LEARNING

The reforms to social work education which we covered in chapter 1 have led to significant changes in the assessment of social work students. To understand the current framework for assessment in practice learning, it is important to explore the context of these changes.

In the recent past, competence based assessment was the preferred method for assessing social work students. Fletcher (1992) defined competence based assessment as *"the generation and collection of evidence of performance which can be matched to specified (and explicit) standards which reflect expectations of performance in the workplace."*

Over the years, competence based assessment came under increasing criticism, for a number of reasons:

Reduction of the role: Social work is a complex and ever changing activity which involves practitioners using knowledge, skills and values in practice in a flexible and creative manner. The National Occupational Standards used with competency based assessment focussed predominantly on tasks and were criticised as reducing the social work role to a series of tasks to be completed.

Tick box approach: There were concerns that practice educators and students had started to approach the assessment of social work practice in a mechanistic manner - reflected in a "tick box" approach to assessment.

Focus on assessment at the expense of learning: where competence based approaches have been used, there is a risk that students and practice educators focus on simply meeting the standards required. This can impede the opportunities for the students to learn from their experiences.

Lack of focus on progress: competence based assessment focuses on whether a student has met the required standard - it does not track the journey that the student has on placement - not does it evidence growth and development. The question is simply "can they do it now?"

What? at the expense of why? and how?: the criticism is that competence based approaches consider what people can do, without exploring how they do it and why they do it in that way.

Focus on ease of assessment: What is really important in professional practice is not necessarily easy to measure and assess. On the other hand, what is easy to assess is not necessarily particularly important in professional practice. Many of the reforms in social work education, particularly those which relate to assessment, can be described as *"making what is important assessable, rather than making what is assessable important"* (Barcham 2012).

The Social Work Task Force and subsequent Reform Board recognised these criticisms and set out a series of reforms in social work education to ensure that social work graduates felt able to practice confidently and safely. These reforms changed the context of assessment in social work practice learning in three main ways:

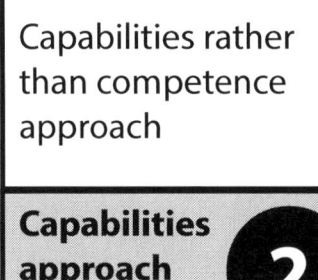

Subsequent chapters in this section explore these issues in some detail.

IN SUMMARY

In the recent past, existing frameworks in social work education and training came under significant criticism - particularly in relation to the use of National Occupational Standards and competence based approaches to assessment. The contemporary framework of practice learning has addressed these criticisms and perhaps the most significant changes that recent reforms have brought about are in relation to the assessment of students in practice learning environments.

21 USING A PROFESSIONAL FRAMEWORK

Understanding the move from an occupational framework to a professional framework underpins the reforms to social work education and addresses many of the criticisms of previous approaches to student assessment outlined in Chapter 20.

The National Occupational Standards which were in use in the social work degree for over ten years, were made up of six key roles, broken down into 21 units which described *"the functions of social workers"* (Skills for Care 2008). These standards were used as "competences" to be addressed. There was substantial criticism within the sector that the standards were devised largely by employers and that they focussed on tasks - representing social work as an occupation rather than a profession and promoting procedurally based practice.

The Professional Capabilities Framework (PCF) is a professional, as opposed to occupational framework. There has been a longstanding debate about what constitutes a profession as opposed to an occupation. In reviewing the literature, we like to use the following acronym, to understand what makes a profession and therefore how social work is a profession, rather than an occupation.

C: Collegiate. By this we mean having a feeling of belonging to a professional group. Social workers belong to a Global profession, as recognised in the first domain of the PCF.

A: Autonomy balanced with accountability. Professionals have a level of autonomy but recognise that this is balanced with accountability.

S: Skills. A profession involves a defined set of skills.

E: Education. Professionals receive an agreed professional education and are committed to continual professional development.

S: Service user focussed. Professionals should focus on the needs and interests of service users, rather than the organisation.

The PCF recognises social work as a complex profession and builds on the international definition of social work as a profession which:

"promotes social change, problem solving in human relationships and the empowerment and liberation of people to enhance well-being. Utilising theories of human behaviour and social systems, social work intervenes at the points where people interact with their environments. Principles of human rights and social justice are fundamental to social work." (IFSW and IASSW 2000)

At the time of writing, the international definition of social work is under review. The current draft reading as:

"The social work profession facilitates social change and development, social cohesion, and the empowerment and liberation of people. Principles of social justice, human rights, collective responsibility and respect for diversities are central to social work. Underpinned by theories of social work, social sciences, humanities and indigenous knowledge, social work engages people and structures to address life challenges and enhance wellbeing. (IFSW 2013)

The Professional Capabilities Framework was one of nine products developed by the Social Work Reform Board to improve outcomes for service users and carers. It is the sole framework for professional development in social work in England and provides a comprehensive framework for professional development across all areas of social work practice regardless of the professional setting or service user focus. The framework is designed to show and enable progression through career levels and is based on capability rather than competence.

It is important to recognise that the PCF is a professional framework and as such, should be used by all social work professionals to:

- ✓ Direct professional activity
- ✓ Support effective supervision
- ✓ Plan professional development
- ✓ Support re-registration
- ✓ Progress

The PCF is made up of nine domains (aspects of practice) as follows:

1. Professionalism
2. Values and ethics
3. Diversity
4. Rights, justice and economic well-being
5. Knowledge
6. Critical reflection and analysis
7. Intervention and skills
8. Context and organisations
9. Professional leadership

The nine domains are closely related, and as such, they should be viewed as interdependent, rather than separate. The framework makes clear that understanding of what a social worker does will only be complete by taking into account all nine capabilities (TCSW 2012).

In addition to the nine domains, the PCF contains nine levels which reflect professional progression. The first four levels relate to students - demonstrating the significant progress that should take place during qualifying training.

Exactly how each University will use the PCF in practice learning and across their programme generally will vary, and assessment criteria for practice learning will also need to cover the HCPC Standards of Proficiency. However, the College of Social Work (2013) make clear that there are a number of benefits in using the PCF to underpin the assessment of students on placement. These include:

- giving more scope to the judgement of the practice educator about a student's suitability to practice

- providing clearer shared national standards about what is expected of students at different points in their development, highlighting the elements of progression that are significant

- enabling clearer identification by the practice educator of the areas that students need to work on to demonstrate their practice

- introducing students to the framework for professional development that will be used throughout their career as a social worker

The capabilities approach

The move from using competencies to drawing on capability is a significant change in social work education generally. It is not simply a "play on words" but is about a culture shift in terms of understanding what social workers do and what the profession should be about.

The following table illustrates some of the key differences between competence based and capabilities based approaches:

Competence based approaches	Capabilities based approaches
Focuses on what people do and whether this meets standards	Focuses on *how* people do things and *why* they do it in that way
Is about roles and tasks	Is about professional practice
Encourages the student to focus on the requirements of assessment and targets	Encourages the student to focus on their development as a practitioner
Is about routine and details process and procedure	Is about how practice is analysed, evaluated and improved
Is like following a map (Lester 1999)	Is like a student developing their own map and becoming a map maker (Lester 1999)

Lawson (2013) claims that a capabilities approach *"allows social workers to show, and assessors to assess, how relationships are formed, professional judgements are made and how practice is adapted to the context in which the social worker is working."* This encourages a richer, more textured approach to assessing professional practice.

Lester's (1999) assertion that a competence based approach is like following a map, whereas a capabilities approach introduces the idea that the learner is the map maker is very well known and is used as a common analogy to explain a capabilities approach. Building on the College of Social Work's analogy that holistic assessment is like eating a meal (see page 117), I like to think of the student I am working with cooking the meal that we eat together when I assess them. A competence based approach provided students with a range of ready-made meals that they simply had to put in the microwave and press the button before serving it up. A capabilities approach, on the other hand, calls for a student to develop a range of recipes for themselves, looking at the ingredients to hand and then developing creative ways of working with these to serve up a nutritious and satisfying meal. Essentially, the capabilities approach allows for far more creativity and diversity than the previous competence based approaches which were much more reductionist and directive.

IN SUMMARY

The Professional Capabilities Framework provides a clear structure for the development of social work professional practice from the point of entry to qualifying training throughout a social worker's career. This professional framework will inform the assessment criteria for practice learning, along with the HCPC Standards of Proficiency.

HOLISTIC ASSESSMENT

Working with the Professional Capabilities Framework and utilising a capabilities approach requires a holistic approach to assessment. Whilst in many ways this is just about best practice in assessment it is a fundamentally different approach to the competence based assessment approaches which have dominated practice learning in the recent past. Understanding the concept of holistic assessment is therefore vitally important in contemporary practice education.

Understanding holistic assessment

Holistic assessment is commonly used in higher education as an approach to assess student progression and where the learning outcomes to be assessed are complex and inter-related (Akubuilo 2012). Social work is undoubtedly a complex activity made up of an inter-relationship of knowledge, skills and values and social work students are expected to make significant progress during qualifying training. Therefore holistic assessment is the best approach for social work practice learning.

To explain holistic assessment, the College of Social Work (2012a) provides an analogy of eating a meal:

"A holistic assessment is made when the meal is judged on its overall taste, quality and presentation etc. However, if one part of the preparation or an ingredient is missing or below standard, then this will impair the quality of the final product."

This analogy highlights the difference between competence based and capabilities focussed assessment. When eating a meal, you don't watch the cook and tick off a series of tasks to decide how the meal tastes. You eat the meal, decide how it tastes (good or bad) and then think about what made it taste that way. Essentially that is a simple way of understanding holistic assessment of social work practice – the practice educator considers the student's practice overall (is it good or poor practice?) and then reflects on what has influenced their view of this practice (what makes the practice good or poor?)

Recent reports into social work practice (eg: Munro 2011) stress the need for social workers to undertake assessments in a way which helps them to obtain a holistic understanding of needs, recognising the importance of professional judgement. The move towards holistic assessment of students therefore reflects a move towards holistic assessment more generally within the profession.

Implementing holistic assessment

Huba and Freed (2000) argue that holistic assessment is the process of gathering and discussing information from multiple and diverse sources in order to develop a deep understanding of what students know, what they understand and what they can do with their knowledge as a result of their learning experiences. Until practice educators are familiar with holistic assessment it can feel like a very abstract concept. When people are new to a task they often look for concrete approaches ("what do I have to do?")

Holistic assessment calls for a reflective approach to assessment and as such the process of reflection outlined on page 63 can be helpful in providing a more concrete framework for considering how to implement holistic assessment in practice learning situations:

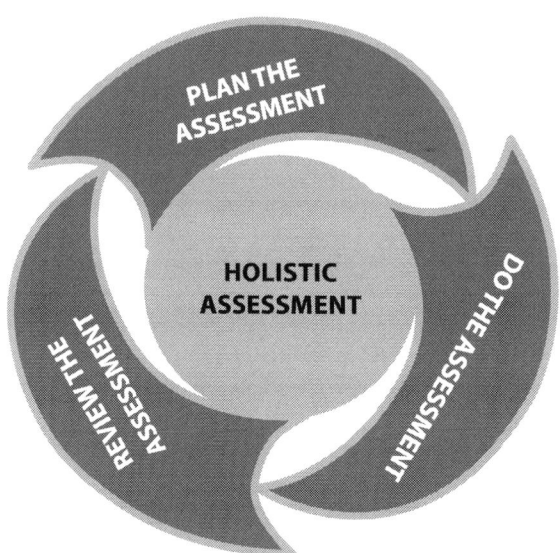

Assessment Planning

If assessment is to be fair and reliable, students must be clear about what is being assessed and how it will be assessed. Where problems arise in assessment it can usually be traced back to problems in the planning stages.

The National Organisation of Practice Teaching Code of Practice states that a practice educator should ensure that:

4.1 There is an agreed understanding about the purpose of assessment and about the methods by which the assessment of the Professional Capabilities Framework is carried out, according to the levels required by the degree programme.

4.2 The student is encouraged to fully contribute to the planning of the assessment process and the time-scale within which the work will be assessed.

(NOPT 2013)

Assessment issues will generally be covered in the learning agreement. However, whilst this provides a general overview of the assessment more detailed planning will take place in supervision about specific assessment activities (for example in preparation for a direct observation).

"Doing" the assessment

A range of assessment methods can be used in assessing the student holistically – see chapter 23. In undertaking the assessment you will also need to consider the following issues:

- Assessing the detail
- Adopting a researchers' mindset
- Working in partnership
- Understanding and using both formative and summative assessment
- Ensuring that assessment promotes learning and that our approach recognises the links between the two

Getting into the detail

A misunderstanding of holistic assessment is that it is a generalised approach which does not get into the detail of specific criteria. However, whilst you will consider the student's practice and progress holistically, there will be times when you need to 'drill down' using the detail of the practice learning assessment criteria. This might relate to those assessment criteria which are the most important in the placement setting or might be where you have particular concerns about the student's practice.

When drilling into the detail:

- Make sure that you are clear with the studen
- Match the methods of assessment to what y observation provides clear practice based evidence whilst supervision discussion and critical reflections provide clear evidence of knowledge and understanding

Adopting a researcher's mindset

Where social workers may be more familiar with process driven assessment practice, it can be useful to think of holistic assessment as more like research than assessment.

Effectively, in holistic assessment, you are researching the 'quality' of a student's practice. You do need to be clear about what they can do, but a holistic approach to assessment is about exploring how they do it and why they do it that way. A range of assessment methods can be used to research the quality of the student's practice - as are outlined in Chapter 23. Many of the approaches used in holistic assessment are drawn from research (for example, direct observations and triangulation). It is therefore easy to consider holistic assessment as researching the quality of a student's practice.

Working in partnership

Good social work practice is based on a partnership approach. Assessment in practice learning is no different. There are three key stakeholders in the assessment process:

- The student
- The practice educator
- Service users

The practice educator needs to promote partnership between all the stakeholders in order to ensure effective assessment practice.

Formative and summative assessment

Formative assessment: describes the assessment activities that take place on an ongoing basis throughout the placement. These activities involve partnership between the student and practice educator. As such, formative assessments also have intrinsic learning value.

Summative assessment: describes the "final" stage of an assessment process. Summative assessments take a snapshot approach - indicating where a student is at the point of assessment. Focussing entirely on using summative assessment therefore leads to a lack of opportunities for learning.

Formative assessments influence the summative assessment - so that nothing comes as a surprise but the summative assessment is where the professional judgement is made, recorded and ultimately "processed".

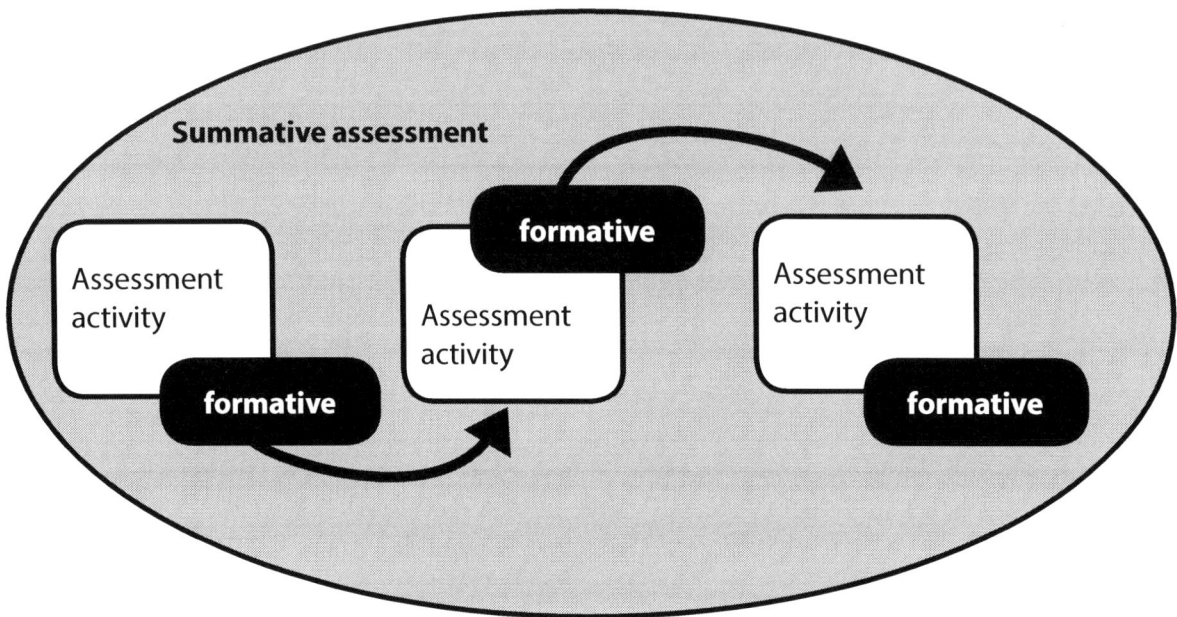

Linking learning and assessment

In education learning cannot be separated from good quality assessment. As Rowntree (1987:24) asserts *"assessment is the life-blood of learning"*. Holistic approaches to assessment recognise and build on these links. Competence based assessment can encourage a surface approach to learning (see page 62) where students work towards meeting set criteria and then move on to looking at the next "box to be ticked". A holistic approach to assessment encourages deeper learning by highlighting the way that the whole can only be seen in light of the parts and the parts can only be judged in terms of the whole. This enables students to explore more fully the complex nature of social work.

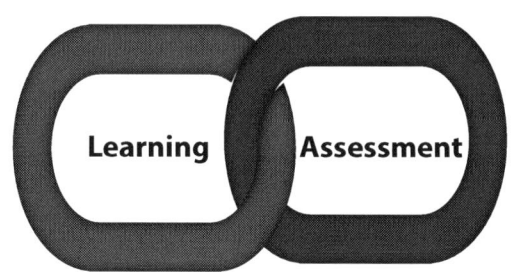

Reviewing the assessment

At all stages of the placement experience you need to review the assessment of the student. Take a reflective approach to reviewing the process of the assessment. Think about:

- What is working and what isn't?
- Are any specific needs the student has being considered and addressed?
- Are you using all the available sources of evidence?
- What does the evidence tell you?
- Is the student making progress?
- Have you planned the assessment effectively and is the plan kept under review?
- How does the student feel about the assessment process and outcomes?
- How do you know the student feels that way?

The remaining chapters in this section will help you to consider how you should review the assessment.

IN SUMMARY

Holistic assessment is a new approach to assessing students. It reflects the move away from procedural assessment practice in social work. Essentially, holistic assessment is about good practice in assessment – following a clear and transparent assessment process can assist in implementing holistic assessment.

23 USING EVIDENCE IN YOUR ASSESSMENT

Holistic assessments need to be evidence based and textured with a variety of evidence. Using triangulation to identify and gather evidence is particularly useful in adopting a holistic approach. The model is based on the following triangle of assessment methods, or evidence sources.

Observation of Practice
(including direct observation and less commonly video and audio evidence)

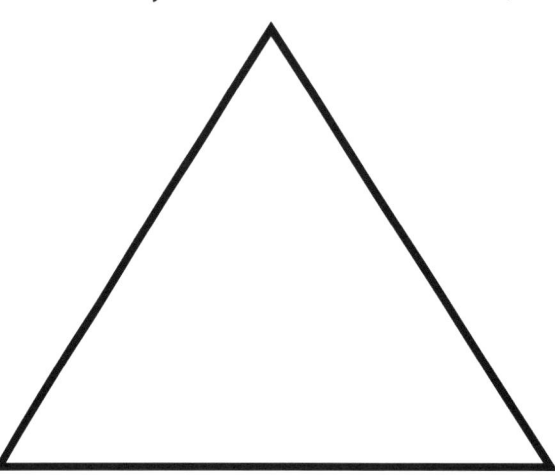

Testimonial Evidence
(feedback – preferably written - can be provided by a variety of people eg: team colleagues, service user, carer, co-worker, other professionals)

Product Evidence
(including general agency recording, letters, supervision notes and assignments - essentially anything that is a product of the work)

In considering the work a student has done, each corner of the triangle should be considered in terms of identifying relevant evidence eg:

- Observation of practice – was this observed or can an observation be arranged?
- Testimonial evidence – who has seen the student do this and how can we get feedback from them?
- Product evidence – what record is there of the work?

Observation is always the strongest source of evidence as it is easy to apply the VACS rules of evidence (see page 127). However, it may not always be possible or appropriate to observe certain areas of practice. The two other corners of the triangle should then be considered. This chapter explores the three sources of evidence and considers the way that triangulation supports holistic assessment.

Direct Observation

Direct observation always includes at least three parties: the student, the practice educator and the service user(s) or carer(s) with whom the student is engaged. Each party has a different role to play in the observation. It is important to remember that where service users are involved their needs necessarily take priority over those of the student and practice educator.

The Potential of Direct Observation

Direct observation of practice has many benefits. In fact, it can be so helpful to all involved that where direct observations of practice have been carried out as part of other qualifications, people continue to arrange occasional observations even after any assessment has concluded.

For students, direct observation provides opportunities to:

- Reflect upon their practice
- Benefit from the practice educator's perspective on the student's work
- Demonstrate capability and receive confirmation of their abilities
- Identify areas of difficulty and obtain advice and support

For practice educators, direct observation provides opportunities to:

- Understand the student's current abilities
- Identify areas for further work and provide relevant learning opportunities
- Obtain evidence to inform their professional judgement and assessment

For service users, direct observation has the potential to:

- Act as a safeguard, through the scrutiny of a student's work by a more experienced practitioner (the practice educator)
- Improve the service received
- Create an opportunity to evaluate the service received and give feedback

(Adapted from University of York 2000)

Practical Issues

Observations need to be carefully planned with students. It is important to remember that students may be particularly anxious about being observed and this needs to be clearly discussed. Where a student is clear about what you are looking for in an observation their anxiety will be better managed. This demonstrates the importance of thoughtful and effective assessment planning.

Remember that the service user/carer must always give permission for the observation. Where they are used to your presence this may be easier to negotiate. However, as a general rule the student is responsible for getting permission from the service user and explaining your role as an observer. Service users who have a good understanding of the observation process are less likely to be distracted by the practice educator's presence.

It is important to remember though, that in any direct observation of practice, the presence of the observer (the practice educator) is likely to have an impact on the situation.

A useful model for the direct observation of practice has been developed for social work students by the University of York (2000).

It focuses on a collaborative approach, whereby the student takes a lead role in the setting of goals, objectives and future learning. It is described as an empowering approach which encourages close and meaningful partnership between the student and their assessor.

The model divides the direct observation into three stages:

Before the observation, the student and the observer meet together to plan the observation, during which time they negotiate and agree:

- a set of assessment objectives. The model suggests that the observer and the student identify 2/3 objectives each.
- what they want to get/give feedback on. These can be areas that need development or where the student needs affirmation of good practice.

The observation takes place with the observer focussing on the objectives agreed in the planning stage.

After the observation the student and observer meet together to discuss how it went. The feedback remains focussed on the objectives which were agreed at Stage 1.

- The student is invited to give their evaluation first - they identify what went well, not so well and what they have learned.
- The observer follows, giving their evaluation.
- The feedback session is concluded with a reflective discussion, based around four areas:
  - surprises
  - satisfactions
  - dissatisfactions
  - learning

Both the student and practice educator can share their thoughts using these broad areas. I find this can provide a useful structure to discussions following the observation. For example, when discussing surprises I can gauge whether there were any changes to the situation based on my presence. When discussing satisfaction and dissatisfaction I also get an idea about whether what I have observed is at the same standard as the student's usual practice etc.

Direct observation evidence can be supplemented by video or audio evidence of practice.

<u>Video Evidence</u>

Whilst video evidence can be used, it is fraught with difficulties such as:

- obtaining the necessary equipment
- ethical issues about videoing service users and associated confidentiality concerns
- students can find videoing uncomfortable

Since there are so many inherent difficulties we would recommend that video evidence is used only in exceptional circumstances when discussed and agreed with the University and all players involved.

<u>Audio Evidence</u>

Again audio evidence of practice has ethical dilemmas in terms of service user involvement, and needs to be carefully considered and discussed before being used.

Feedback from Others

Also referred to as third party feedback, testimonial evidence or witness testimony, this can be a strong source of evidence.

It is always important to negotiate the form feedback should take with students. On the whole written feedback is preferable and some Universities provide a pro forma for this.

Feedback can be sought from a range of people:

- *Feedback from Service Users*

Feedback from people who use social work services is of central importance, not only in terms of assessment, but also in encouraging learning and professional development

There can be obvious problems inherent in service user feedback. For example, the power dynamics of the service user/student relationship can have a significant impact on the feedback. However, it is important to involve service users in the assessment process and this is now more widely recognised.

"The learning that can be achieved through service user and carer involvement in assessment is not just important for the development of individuals but also for the development of a culture in which whole organisations 'learn' to understand and be more responsive to the needs and wishes of its service users."

(Williams and Rutter 2007:121)

The form that service user feedback takes and the method for collecting it will vary, so it is important to negotiate with the student as early as possible about the options for gaining service user feedback. I generally ask students to develop a feedback plan towards the end of their induction period. I ask students to reflect on the importance of feedback, the barriers they might face and what strategies they can use to overcome these barriers. I find that developing this feedback plan helps students to recognise the central importance of feedback from service users in developing good practice.

It can also be a useful learning experience to ask a student to design a form to give to service users to obtain feedback. On the face of it, this sounds a fairly straightforward task. However, there is a great deal to be learnt from this task – about communication, service user involvement and empowerment etc.

Of course, there may be situations where obtaining a service user's feedback will be more difficult – for example where service users do not communicate verbally. Those who know the service user (eg: an advocate) may be able to advise or provide feedback. Carers (eg: a service user's family and friends) may also be able to give feedback in this situation. It is also important to recognise that feedback might be provided both formally and informally. Creativity is important in gaining service user feedback.

- *Feedback from Colleagues*

Often, colleagues are in a strong position to provide feedback on a student's practice. They may, for example, have worked alongside a student on an aspect of work relating to the standards.

- *Feedback from Other Professionals*

Other professionals can provide a good source of evidence for some standards. However, it is important to remember that other professionals may not have a full understanding of the role of a social worker so the feedback may need to be weighed against this.

General Guidance

Feedback is only helpful where it is clear and relevant in some way to the assessment criteria. It may be very pleasant for a student to receive written feedback saying they are "a very good worker", but what exactly does that mean? Whoever seeks the feedback (usually the student) needs to be very clear about what they are looking for, so that the evidence produced is useful and relevant.

Product Evidence

Product evidence basically refers to anything that has been produced by the student as part of their work.

Students will routinely complete case recording, they may also write letters and reports. All of these can be strong sources of evidence. The practice educator should have routine access to agency documentation completed by the student and this evidence should be discussed as part of the assessment process.

Using the Full Range of Available Evidence

As a student progresses through a placement, a whole range of evidence from the different sources discussed in this chapter will be available. Remember also that supervision discussion will provide evidence of the student's capability and understanding – so supervision notes provide a good source of 'product' evidence.

To avoid error in assessment it is important to use as wide a range of assessment methods as possible. This also ensures that the assessment is fair and that the opportunities for the student to demonstrate capable practice are maximised.

IN SUMMARY

A range of assessment methods and evidence sources can be used in making an assessment of a student. Students may need advice and support to identify appropriate evidence and the triangulation model can be useful here. Fair and reliable holistic assessment will involve the use of a wide range of assessment methods.

24 PROFESSIONAL JUDGEMENT AND ASSESSMENT DECISIONS

Holistic assessment practice relies on the professional judgement of the practice educator. Clearly this means that practice educators need to be accountable for the decisions they make and for the way they undertake the assessment process. As a practice educator you will want to take a number of issues into account in reaching decisions and making assessment recommendations:

Evaluating the quality of evidence

A wide range of evidence will be generated during the placement period. This will need to be carefully considered and evaluated. The VACS criteria is often used to critically evaluate evidence, as follows:

*V*alidity – the key question a practice educator must ask when considering each piece of evidence is "what does this evidence tell me?" It may tell you something about the particular aspect of practice being assessed or it may tell you about some other work activity.

*A*uthenticity – if a student is to be seen as capable, there must be no doubt that the evidence relates to that individual's own work. Where evidence relates to joint working, this is particularly important and the practice educator will need to check out with the other person/people involved which part of the work is the student's own.

*C*onsistency – holistic assessment is about drawing on evidence which reflects the student's practice over a period of time. As a general rule evidence should 'date' across the placement period, so that not all the evidence is drawn from one day, one piece of work etc.

*S*ufficiency – sufficient evidence needs to be collected to demonstrate beyond all reasonable doubt that the student has performed to the required standard. This can create difficulties for practice educators in terms of "how much is enough?" Practice educators should use practice educator support meetings to help them answer this question. It is important to remember that a student does not need to present a 'new' piece of evidence for each aspect of practice being considered. In fact one piece of evidence can provide evidence of a range of practice. If students had to produce new evidence for each assessment criteria, then students and practice educators would be pushing portfolios round in wheelbarrows!

Each programme will provide guidance on the amount and types of evidence they require (for example they will provide guidance on how many direct observations of practice should take place). Practice educators will need to assess sufficiency in relation to specific programme requirements.

Recognising the context of the decision

According to O'Grady (2004) in holistic assessment practice "students are still judged against general criteria… but in the measurement….. of each student … *how* they *understand* is contextualised into the professional judgement." Therefore the practice educator needs to make their assessment decision drawing on the student's progress and development, their understanding about their own practice, the context of the organisation and placement setting and the level of the PCF being considered. A great deal therefore needs to be taken into account by the practice educator.

Ensuring the decision is evidence based

Assessment decisions need to take the whole breadth and depth of evidence generated during the placement into account. Triangulating assessments (see chapter 23) can assist in ensuring bith the breadth and depth of evidence. All the documentation which grows out of the placement experience should be used to evidence progression, any concerns, the student's approach to the assessment and what they have learnt from reflecting on the assessment activities.

Taking a critically reflective approach

Decisions which are informed by reflection are always more robust and defensible. This reinforces the need for practice educators to take a reflective approach to their assessment responsibilities.

Consistency

Taking all these issues into account in making an assessment decision should ensure that the practice educator's professional judgment is reliable.

It is important to ensure that:

- Two different practice educators would make the same decision about the same student (technically referred to as inter-rater reliability). Involving others in aspects of the assessment of the student (for example seeking feedback from others, involving a colleague in carrying out a direct observation etc) assists in ensuring consistency and reliability of judgements.

- A practice educator would make the same decision about the same practice if it were repeated (technically referred to as intra-rater reliability).The danger is that on different days you might view things differently or you might view similar practice carried out by different students very differently. Being mindful in your assessment practice can avoid these dangers and ensure reliability.

IN SUMMARY

In holistic assessment the professional judgment of the assessor is vital. Those new to practice education can lack confidence in making assessment decisions. Following the basic principles covered in this chapter can assist in making assessment decisions more robust and reliable

25 PROVIDING FEEDBACK

The key to good assessment practice is the provision of good quality feedback in good time. Tsui (2005) asserts that giving feedback to practitioners is an art. It is certainly true that it requires skill to provide effective feedback which enables people to learn from their experience.

Feedback can be either positive (that is, reinforcing good practice) or negative (that is, feedback on poor performance). Both positive and negative feedback can be constructive. Where feedback is constructive it will enable the student to develop their practice. Where feedback is missing or destructive the student will not be able to develop effectively.

Feedback is a vital part of assessment in that feedback, where a student is seen as not yet meeting the requirements of the assessment criteria, will enable the student and the practice educator to review and adapt the assessment plan. Where a student is judged to be meeting the requirements, feedback is still a vital part of the process and will enable the student to plan for their future development beyond the end of the practice learning opportunity and the achievement of the qualification. It is important that students never feel that once they have qualified, they have no more to do. The achievement of any qualification is always part of a continuum of professional development.

Guidelines for Giving Constructive Feedback

Constructive feedback provides information about the student's performance in such a way that the student maintains a positive attitude towards themselves, their placement and the qualification. It encourages students to commit themselves to a personal action plan to progress further. Constructive feedback is intrinsically linked to the process of learning. When you provide effective feedback you are helping the student to learn. The following guidelines will help you to think through what makes feedback constructive and therefore effective.

- **Positive**

  Feedback should always start and finish with a positive. This is often referred to as the positive sandwich. The content of the sandwich gives the student something to work on, whilst the 'bread' is the positive aspects. Providing feedback, using the sandwich technique, builds on motivation and self esteem.

Deal clearly with particular instances and behaviour rather than making vague or sweeping statements. For example "when asking about mobility, you moved too quickly through the questions rather than allowing the person to fully answer". Rather than "your listening skills were poor".

- **Descriptive**

Use descriptive rather than evaluative terms. For example, "my perception was that when you repeated the same question several times the person became confused", rather than "your questioning technique was confusing".

- **Actionable**

Direct feedback towards behaviour that the student can do something about. For example, "if you slowed down your delivery, it would probably be easier for the person to follow what you were saying", rather than "your accent is hard to understand."

- **Prioritised**

Concentrate on the two or three key areas for improvement, preferably including those where the student can see a quick return. Break down a major problem into smaller, step-by-step goals. (This is the 'content' of the positive sandwich).

- **Offer alternatives**

Offer suggestions to what could have been done differently. Turn negatives into a positive. For example, "when you remained seated at the start it seemed unwelcoming. Shaking her hand and smiling might have helped set up a better rapport".

- **Well-timed**

The most useful feedback is given when the student is receptive to it and it is sufficiently close to the event to be fresh in their mind.

- **Facilitative**

Rather than prescribing behaviour, feedback should help the student question their behaviour and encourage them to be more reflective about their practice. For example, "How might that have been interpreted by the service user?"

- **Clear**

Avoid jargon wherever possible and ensure that your communication is clear. Always check feedback to ensure that the student understands you.

It's Not What You Say It's the Way that You Say It!

No doubt, you will have heard this said a number of times. As a competent worker you will be aware of the importance of effective communication. However, it's worth re-visiting this concept in terms of feedback.

Research has shown that what you say contributes only a small part of the message heard by the listener. For example, as long ago as 1967, Mehrabian and Ferris found that:

- What you say (ie: the words used) accounts for 7% of the message received.
- How you say it (ie: the tone of voice, the emphasis given to words and the volume and pace of what you say) accounts for 38% of the message received.
- How you look when you say it (ie: body language – posture, facial expression, eye contact etc) accounts for 55% of the message received.

So, don't forget all your basic communication skills when providing feedback to students!

When Feedback is Difficult

Feedback on assessment decisions can be difficult for a range of reasons. Fears about the responses of students, particularly to negative feedback, can inhibit practice educators in giving accurate feedback. However, it is vital to give honest feedback to students, throughout the practice learning opportunity.

<u>What do I do if the student disagrees with the feedback?</u>

This can be problematic as you won't be able to move on through the assessment until there is some level of agreement between you.

If the student disagrees with the facts you are basing your feedback on then:

- Give detailed examples
- Check the areas of disagreement eg: "Do you think 'it' didn't take place or are you disagreeing about details of 'it'?"
- Clarify the student's version of events and have an open mind

If the student disagrees that a problem exists ("everyone makes mistakes") then explain the consequences of the action. Point out that making mistakes does not constitute competence, so you will need to see positive evidence for the standard in question.

<u>What do I do if they start crying?</u>

If you ensure that your feedback follows the guidelines given, this is unlikely. However, if a student does cry when you are giving them feedback, then:

- Be empathic eg: "I understand you will be shocked if no one has talked to you about this before."
- Give permission for the student to cry (it can relieve stress)
- Talk about why the student is finding the feedback upsetting
- Try not to put off the session. It may be tempting to do so, but if you do, you will be leaving the student with the distress. Try to move on, instead, to finding solutions which will end the session on a positive note.

<u>What do I do if they get angry?</u>

A natural defence mechanism when a person feels under pressure is anger. If a student becomes angry, then:

- Be empathic eg: "I understand why you feel shocked/angry…."
- Find something to say that agrees with the student eg: "I know that you are working hard on this area in difficult circumstances…."
- Don't be put off giving the feedback. The student may be using anger as an avoidance technique.

IN SUMMARY

The provision of constructive feedback is a vital aspect of assessing a student's practice. Giving feedback constructively is a skill – practice educators and others involved in the provision of practice learning should seek to develop this skill further.

26 COMMON SOURCES OF ERROR IN THE ASSESSMENT OF COMPETENCE

As we have covered, it is vitally important that assessment of social work practice is transparent, holistic and draws on a range of assessment methods. However, even where assessment practice takes these issues into account, there can be errors in the assessment of students. These include:

Halo/Horns Effect

The 'Halo' effect involves practice educators inferring good practice on the part of a student on the basis of previous good performance by that student, without him/her actually being required to demonstrate the performance to the current standard. The previous performance may not have been associated with the criteria now being assessed.

The 'Horns' effect is similar to the halo effect, only the opposite. On the basis of previous unsatisfactory performance by the student an expectation exists that future performances will also be unsatisfactory. Instead of waiting for the performance, the practice educator infers (possibly wrongly) that these future performances will be unsatisfactory.

Crediting 'Nice' People

This is about crediting those who in everyday life strike us as pleasant/nice people who we warm to and want to spend time with. It is common to make the jump from liking them not just on the basis of a casual contact but perhaps on the basis of more established contact to inadvertently 'conspiring' with them to help them through the assessment.

The opposite can happen just as easily!

Stereotyping

Stereotyping is always dangerous and directly contravenes the professional value base. In relation to assessment, stereotyping can occur in terms of assuming a certain level of capability (or lack of capability) based on an apparent characteristic of a student.

It is not only the assumption itself which is dangerous, but also the way in which it might lead a practice educator to look for certain pieces of evidence.

> Remember, whenever we assume it makes an ASS out of U and ME

First Impressions

This involves a practice educator 'taking a liking' to a student (or the opposite) and on the basis of this first or early contact viewing the student's performance more or less favourably than should be the case.

If you imagine a student who is warm and welcoming when you first meet him/her you can also imagine how difficult it is to be objective, especially if being objective means perhaps jeopardising that warmth.

Giving More Weight to the Negatives than the Positives

This occurs where a student has performed in a manner contrary to that required by the standard on one occasion – perhaps in very significant area of work. In order to be satisfied that s/he is meeting the criteria and the need for consistency, a practice educator may then expect many more evidence than is necessary before they agree the student is capable. Getting the balance right is vital.

Inferring or Generalising

Don't work on the basis that 'because the student can do A, s/he can also do B, C and D'.

Similar to Me

This involves judging a student favourably because they carry out a piece of work like we would or have values which are just like ours. 'Ours' may be the wrong way or not the required way! It is also important to remember that there are often many ways of carrying out a task. Just because a student does something in a different way to you doesn't mean they are not a capable professional.

Contrast Effects

This arises when one student's performance is compared to that of another student by a practice educator. The inferior performance may then be deemed not capable, no matter how it stands compared to the assessment criteria and evidence requirements. Students must be assessed against criteria, not against each other. This is an error which is often seen in team environments – for example team members often compare one student to a student the team has worked with before. This can impact on any feedback they provide to the practice educator.

BEWARE OF DIRECTLY COMPARING PERFORMANCE

Benefit of the Doubt

Where a performance has not conclusively met the criteria being assessed or fully provided the evidence which is required, this error involves giving the student the "benefit of the doubt". Agreeing that s/he is competent on the basis of what evidence is provided – insufficient as it is.

If you are not sure that the evidence has been provided don't side with the student – err on the side of caution. Be conservative in your judgement – make sure.

Experimenter Effect

If you're not generally around the student when they are working, then your observing him/her will probably intimidate the student – your presence influences the performance. We all do strange things when we are intimidated! This may also have an effect on the way others involved in the observation (eg: service users, colleagues) act. This can also affect the student's performance. One way to check that the experimenter effect hasn't been an issue is to ask the student after an observation "Did anything surprise you?" (See page 124)

Excessive Demands for Evidence

Make sure that the precise evidence which you are looking for, is neither inadequate nor excessive. Make a judgement on what is the right amount of evidence, in partnership with the student based on the assessment requirements in the programme. Check this out with the student's tutor, with other practice educators at meetings etc. Once capability is demonstrated it is wasteful to ask for more demonstrations of the performance, and frustrating to the student. Excessive demands are equally as damaging to assessment as insufficient demands.

Not Understanding the Standards

Unless you are thoroughly familiar with the assessment criteria and standards required within the student's specific programme, you will not be able to help students to understand what is required of them, nor identify whether the evidence produced matches that which is required.

The best way of coming to an understanding of the standards is by discussing them with practice learning colleagues in support groups and by talking to University tutors and practice learning co-ordinators.

Reductionist / tick box approach

As we covered in Chapter 20 there have been various criticisms of competence based assessment. Where practice educators and supervisors are experienced in working with students, they may continue to assess in a reductionist way. For example, they may misunderstand the reforms to social work education and see the revised practice learning assessment criteria as simply a new set of competencies to 'ticked off'. The revised assessment criteria should not be seen as separate tasks or skills. Aspects of practice to be assessed should be seen as closely linked and inter-related.

IN SUMMARY

A range of errors can occur in the assessment process. Any of these errors can occur at any stage of the assessment process. Practice Assessment Panels, moderation activities etc are all efforts to keep the possibilities of error to a minimum. It is important to recognise that such error is inevitable in complex social relationships, such as those which exist where people are being assessed, and to guard against it.

27 COMPLETING THE ASSESSMENT

So far this section has considered the assessment process and how you can work to support a student in generating appropriate evidence of their progress and capability. What we haven't considered so far, is how the assessment is recorded and completed.

Every University will have their own system of documentation. As a minimum, you should expect to be provided with:

- A format for recording observations of practice
- A format or pro forma for the final report (and if applicable, the mid placement report)

It is vital that you use the documentation provided by the student's University and that you follow whatever requirements the programme has. Programmes vary in their requirements about:

- Exactly how they draw up the assessment criteria using the HCPC standards of proficiency and the PCF.
- What academic work (eg: assignments, analysis of practice etc) the student will need to complete as part of the assessment process
- How many observations of practice need to be carried out
- What documentation needs to be completed as part of the assessment (eg: mid placement report, final report) etc.
- What has to be provided at the end of a placement (eg: is a portfolio required? What should the portfolio contain?)
- Other assessment requirements (eg: some require service user feedback to be specifically recorded etc).

You must ensure that you follow these requirements. This chapter will provide some prompts about completing the assessment but ensure that you are familiar with the specific programme requirements.

Placement Documentation

It will be clear by now that a range of documentation is produced during any practice learning opportunity. We would also strongly advise practice educators and supervisors to also keep a rolling contact record.

This is very similar to the contact sheet used by many agencies for recording contacts with service users. It can be a hand written document or easily created on a PC by using a table in a Word document or similar. The purpose of it is several fold:

- To record basic discussions and agreements made with the student where there are no other means of recording these
- To hold a record of issues where concerns begin to be identified about the student, team or individual

- To record details of dates of significant events that may later identify a pattern of absenteeism or continued late arrival
- The baseline from which a student's journey begins and how they progress subsequently

It is not intended for the practice educator to be suspicious of the student from the outset, but experience has demonstrated that a record kept like this from the outset, has been invaluable in many situations.

REMEMBER – it is only basic notes, it should not replace the supervision recording and should be done only with the full knowledge of the student.

All of the documentation generated during a placement will be useful in completing the assessment of the student and ensuring a clear evidence base.

Report Writing

Practice educators will need to complete a report at the end of the placement. The requirements for these vary from one programme to another so it is essential that you check programme requirements. Most programmes are willing to provide example reports to assist practice educators with this task. Final reports generally start with the practice educator's recommendation on whether a student has passed or failed the placement. This is clearly the aspect of practice learning which creates the most anxiety for students. It is vital that nothing in the final report comes as a surprise to the student. The student should be kept aware of the progress of the assessment, the practice educator's judgements and how these will inform the final recommendation at all stages of the placement. Students should be involved in the completion of the final report – it is usual that this is an agenda item in supervision for the final few weeks of the placement. As a minimum the student must read the report prior to its submission - they should sign it to show that the report has been shared with them.

Many programmes require a mid placement report to be provided for a meeting mid way through the placement (usually attended by the student, tutor, practice educator and supervisor). The mid placement report will give an indication of the student's progress to date and issues to be addressed in the second half of the placement. It should also indicate whether the student is on track to pass the placement.

Future learning needs

Your assessment report will provide evidence about the student's 'journey' during the placement. It is important to recognise that whilst you will be considering specific assessment criteria for the placement and the student may have reached *a* destination, this is not a final destination. We all have more to learn and to assist students on their future professional journey it is important that you highlight their future learning needs as part of the placement documentation.

Portfolios

Most programmes require the student to submit some kind of portfolio at the completion of the practice learning opportunity. Portfolios vary significantly although they generally bring together evidence of capability. They often contain reflection and documents generated across the placement period. Typical contents include:

- Learning agreement
- Mid placement report
- Final placement report
- Supervision notes
- Student reflections
- Academic work completed during the placement
- Feedback from others
- Reports on direct observation

It is vital that practice educators and students are clear from the outset of the placement about portfolio requirements. Students can become very anxious about the production of a portfolio unless they are clear about both the content and structure. Practice educators need to familiarise themselves with portfolio requirements so that they can provide advice and guidance to students.

Confidentiality

There are a range of confidentiality issues in relation to the assessment of students. It is obviously vital that the names and other identifying features of service users and carers do not appear in any assessment documentation or in a student's portfolio. Programmes should provide guidance on how they expect confidentiality to be maintained – but the most straightforward method is to use an alphabetical code.

Where portfolios require actual evidence of work practice to be included (eg: completed agency documentation, letters written by the student etc) it is vitally important to ensure that the evidence is fully and appropriately anonymised. Agency requirements on Data Protection must be considered. Where students fail to address issues of confidentiality they are directly contravening required professional standards.

General Guidance

It should be clear by now that the best way for practice educators to effectively complete the assessment is for them to keep ongoing records throughout the placement – these will be extremely useful as the placement comes to an end and the report needs to be written, the portfolio needs to be completed etc. Whatever you do, don't leave recording the assessment of the student to the final stages of the placement. Assessment should be an ongoing issue throughout the practice learning opportunity.

Assessment Process Following Practice Learning

Many people feel that when the final report is completed and submitted along with any other required documentation (eg: portfolio) the assessment process is complete. However, at this stage the practice educator's recommendation is still just that – a recommendation. The assessment process within the University needs to be completed. Although different Universities will have slightly different arrangements (for example, some Universities 'sample' at practice assessment panels whilst some read everything in detail) the general framework is as follows:

```
Results of assessments from          At the end of the placement,
    academic modules - eg:           the practice educator makes
                                  recommendation of PASS / FAIL
  • assignments                              practice
  • presentations
  • examinations
```

PRACTICE ASSESSMENT PANEL
Practice educators and tutors read reports / portfolios / assignments and comment on recommendation made eg: agree / disagree

EXTERNAL ASSESSORS
- Act as moderators in considering the marks given to academic work
- Receive any contested placement reports and make final decision
- Read any reports relating to placements where concerns procedures were initiated
- View sample of reports and can overturn decisions

EXAM BOARD
(made up of University staff, External Assessors and Chair of Practice Assessment Panel)
- Discussion on each student
- Ratification of decisions
- At the end of each year recommend progression onto next year
- At end of course recommend Award

It is important for practice educators to be aware of the assessment process following practice learning – as they may well be asked to take part in aspects such as panel attendance. Attending practice assessment panels is always worthwhile as practice educators can learn a great deal from this experience.

IN SUMMARY

All Universities will have their own specific requirements for the completion of the assessment of a student's practice learning. It is vital that practice educators are familiar with this and feel confident about it – where practice educators are unclear this will only serve to heighten any anxieties a student may have.

KEY LEARNING POINTS

- Holistic assessment approaches have now replaced competence based assessment in social work education
- A wide range of assessment methods can be used to assess students in practice learning environments
- Assessment should be student focused and any specific assessment requirements a student may have must be addressed
- Universities have differing requirements for the completion of a student's assessment – practice educators must ensure that they are familiar with these requirements
- Feedback is an essential part of the assessment process – the provision of good quality constructive assessment is also an important aspect of facilitating a student's learning
- A range of errors can occur in the assessment process - practice educators should ensure they work in a way which prevents these occurring

VALUES ISSUES

The professional value base is an essential part of social work practice. Values issues have been incorporated throughout this guide. We have, however, chosen to also include a separate section on values in order to take a "belt and braces" approach to values.

LINKS TO PEPS — ALL DOMAINS

28 THE VALUES FRAMEWORK

The values framework in practice learning is drawn from a number of key documents:

Professional Codes of Practice

The HCPC Standards of conduct, performance and ethics (revised 2012) outline standards for registrants and include aspects of values. Registered social workers will need to meet these standards in their practice.

The British Association of Social Workers revised their code of ethics in 2012. This provides an ethical framework for social work practitioners.

The Professional Capabilities Framework also addresses ethics and values in relation to social work practice.

Social workers working as practice educators and placement supervisors should work in line with the values expressed in these codes / frameworks.

Some supervisors may come from a different professional background and may have their own code of practice. For example, nurses will operate within the Nursing and Midwifery Council Code of Professional Conduct: Standards for conduct, performance and ethics. If people involved in the provision of practice learning are working to different codes of practice, it is a useful exercise to ask students to compare and contrast the different codes of practice as a supervision exercise.

Values for Practice Educators and Supervisors

The statement of values for practice educators, first developed in 2002 by the General Social Care Council, is now included in the Practice Educator Professional Standards. This values statement explores how practice educators and placement supervisors should work to apply social work values to their practice learning roles, as follows:

VALUES FOR PRACTICE EDUCATORS AND SUPERVISORS

In order to promote anti-oppressive and anti-discriminatory practice, practice educators and supervisors will:

- identify and question their own values and prejudices, the use of authority and power in the assessment relationship, and recognise and act upon the implications for their assessment practice;

- update themselves on best practice in assessment and research on adult learning and apply this knowledge in promoting the rights and choices of learners and managing the assessment process;

- respect and value the uniqueness and diversity of learners and recognise and build on their strengths, and take into account individual learning styles and preferred assessment methods;

- accept and respect learners' circumstances and understand how these impact on the assessment process;

- Assess in a manner that does not stigmatise or disadvantage individuals and ensures equality of opportunity. Show applied knowledge and understanding of the significance of:
    - Poverty
    - Racism
    - Ill health and disability
    - Gender
    - Social class
    - Sexual orientation

  in managing the assessment process;

- recognise and work to prevent unjustifiable discrimination and disadvantage in all aspects of the assessment process, and counter any unjustifiable discrimination in ways that are appropriate to their situation and role; and

- take responsibility for the quality of their work and ensure that it is monitored and appraised; critically reflect on their own practice and identify development needs in order to improve their own performance, raise standards, and contribute to the learning and development of others.

(TCSW 2012b)

Code of Practice for Practice Educators

The National Organisation for Practice Teaching has a code of practice specifically for practice educators. Revised in 2013, this code of practice has values issues integrated throughout; particularly helpful is the opening statement on anti-oppressive and anti-discriminatory practice.

ANTI-OPPRESSIVE/ANTI-DISCRIMINATORY STATEMENT

In promoting anti-oppressive/anti-discriminatory practice, practice educators and practice supervisors should:

- Take responsibility for their own learning through questioning their assumptions, values and prejudices and consider the effect of these on their own individual experience and practice.

- Acknowledge the power imbalance within the practice educator/ student relationship and the potential for discrimination this creates.

- Encourage students to recognise and work towards minimising the effects of structural inequality and injustice.

- Demonstrate in their own practice, the principles of anti-oppressive/ anti-discriminatory practice.

- Enable students to identify, analyse and counter discrimination in a manner which takes account of their role and context.

- Involve the service user in the development and assessment of the student's learning wherever practicable.

NOPT (2013)

The remainder of this section covers some of the values issues, dilemmas and conflicts which can occur within practice learning. As a practice educator, you are responsible for facilitating the student's learning in relation to values, helping the student integrate values into their practice and assessing the student's values in practice. As such, it is vital that you act as a role model in terms of your application of professional values in your practice education role.

The aspects of values covered in this section are not exhaustive but will help you to consider how the professional values you work with everyday can be integrated into your work with a student.

IN SUMMARY

Professional values are always informed by a framework of statements. The value base for practice education is informed by a range of statements and codes of practice. Practice educators and supervisors should operate within these codes at all times.

29 POWER AND PRACTICE LEARNING

The process of practice learning creates an unequal role relationship – that of the practice educator and student and to some extent (if applicable) the supervisor and student (essentially the assessor and the assessed). The practice educator occupies an authority role which is intrinsically more powerful.

People being assessed may feel resistant to the assessment process and much of this is about power dynamics. They may also fear or feel hostile towards the practice educator. Past experiences influence expectations and students who bring with them painful or unjust experiences of learning and assessment, may find the prospect of practice learning particularly daunting. Students with visible or invisible differences which could make them the target of discrimination may have specific concerns about being treated fairly (see Chapter 30).

In order to work effectively with the power differentials inherent in the practice learning process, it is important to have a clear understanding of the different forms of power within practice learning arrangements:

- **Professional / Expert Power**

    As the student is a learner whilst the practice educator is a professional – often a very experienced and additionally qualified worker, the practice educator will be seen as the expert. The professional opinion of practice educators is likely to be given more weight than that of the student, for example, and this can lead to a student feeling powerless. Students who have previous working experience can feel this aspect of power differential particularly keenly. They may have previously held professional power and now feel that they have lost this, they may feel particularly de-skilled and a practice educator needs to be aware of this and discuss the experiences and feelings of the student sensitivity.

    A common example of the way people perceive professional power is when students introduce themselves to service users and other professionals they have responses such as "I don't want to speak to a student….. I want to speak to a proper social worker." Other common comments include "well, he's *only* a student…." Or "she's *just a* student" etc. Most students have experienced comments or responses similar to these, devaluing the student role against that of a worker. If you are working with a student who has an experience like this, it's important to sensitively discuss their feelings and offer support and advice on how best to deal with this.

- **Resource Power**

    Practice educators and supervisors are likely to have more knowledge than the student about local resources, practice learning resources etc. This knowledge can be used to support students to access opportunities or it can be used to withhold learning and assessment opportunities.

- **Societal Power**

    Societal power is basically power derived from the oppression of certain groups in society and status issues. Certainly practice educators and supervisors hold societal power in terms of the way society views power between "teacher" and "learners".

    Other societal power dynamics based on forms of oppression such as racism, sexism and disablism can go either way – so that students may hold some societal power. For example, where a black woman supervisor is working with a white man as a student, the student will hold societal power both in terms of race and gender.

    The Inner London Probation Service (1995) describe this source of power as being derived from "the ideology of superiority" within society. It is therefore easy to see that where this form of power lies will differ in terms of each individual situation. It is useful to discuss this form of power with students to assist in their understanding of oppression within society and within individual relationships.

- **The Power to Determine**

    This is perhaps the issue which is most acute in the student's mind and which separates the power held by practice educators and supervisors. Practice educators are responsible for making a recommendation about whether the student has passed or failed a placement and so "determine" the future of the student (as far as the student is concerned). Whilst feedback from a supervisor and others will inform the practice educator's decision, the student will be aware that the recommendation can only be made by the practice educator. This will have a major impact on the relationship between the student and practice educator.

It can be tempting to deny the power imbalance in a practice learning situation. However, this makes the issue more difficult to manage. Best practice is to discuss the power issues and negotiate how the impact of these will be managed.

Addressing the Power Imbalance

There is always the temptation to ignore power differentials and avoid discussing them, in the misguided belief that discussing power will heighten the student's awareness and make them feel more disempowered. However, students are always aware of the power dynamics; not discussing them will only make students feel more concerned about power.

The same kinds of power differentials exist in every professional relationship – for example, between workers and service users, between different professionals etc. Discussing this with students and explaining that there are similarities in their relationships with service users can be a really useful way of addressing power imbalances. For example, if we return to the sources of power considering relationships between the student and service user:

- Professional/expert power. The service user may well see the student as a professional with expertise

- Resource power – the student is more likely to have knowledge about the resources available to service users

- Societal power – the same differences will exist between students and service users. The student will hold some societal power by the very fact that the service user is a service user and the stigma associated with this

- The power to determine – the student may be carrying out an assessment of the service user and hence will have the power to determine – for example, they may be making a recommendation about whether a service user meets eligibility criteria etc.

Discussing the power dynamics inherent in all professional relationships in this way and asking the student where they feel the power lies, will be a good learning experience for the student and will help you begin to discuss the "safety nets" in place to ensure that power is not abused. For example, everyone working to policies and procedures, codes of practice, the existence of complaints procedures etc all provide a safety net.

Discussing power dynamics is the first step in addressing any negative effects of the power differentials. Other important aspects to ensuring that a student does not feel powerless include:

Empowerment in Assessment

You will be familiar with the principles of empowerment in terms of your professional practice. It is also important that you work in an empowering way with students.

To be empowered, people need to know as much as possible about what is going to happen and why. This shows how important it is to keep the student fully informed and to have an open and transparent approach to practice learning.

Where students have not experienced practice learning before, they are likely to draw comparisons with their previous experiences of education. There is a tradition of being passive in education, of the 'learner' feeling unable to ask questions. Good quality practice education recognises the possibility of students taking on a passive role and attempts to address it by:

- Being clear about the process of practice learning and in particular the assessment of student
- Creating an enabling environment where questions are encouraged and uncertainty is acknowledged and discussed
- Promoting partnership approaches
- Providing accessible and relevant written and verbal information on the practice learning process

You should also work to ensure that the placement is student led as far as possible. This increases the sense of control which students have. In your professional practice, you should be familiar with working in a user-centred way. As a practice educator, you should seek to work in a student led way, whilst recognising that practice learning should also be focussed on service users needs and experiences.

Complaints and Appeals Procedures

All programmes should have a clearly written complaints and appeals procedure. Again, issues of power have a direct bearing, for if students feel that they will face some form of reprimand for complaining they will be reluctant to do so. Students need to be well informed about appeals and complaints procedures and they need to feel confident about using these if they need to.

Be clear with students that they should raise any concerns that they have with the practice educator and/or supervisor as soon as possible. Ensure they know if they raise any concerns that this will not be held against them. Students are generally very reluctant to raise any concerns because they are so aware of the power differentials. It's important to help students feel comfortable and safe to raise any concerns they have.

TECHNIQUES FOR REDUCING THE EFFECTS OF THE POWER IMBALANCE IN PRACTICE LEARNING

- ✓ Discuss power issues rather than denying them
- ✓ Ensure the placement is student led
- ✓ Be clear with the student about practice learning processes and particularly the process of assessment
- ✓ Employ all the principles of fair assessment practice
- ✓ Promote partnership at all times
- ✓ Work to create a safe learning environment where questions are encouraged and uncertainty is acknowledged
- ✓ Employ all the principles of learning empowerment

IN SUMMARY

The power differentials in practice learning are undeniable. It is essential that these are acknowledged and discussed with the student in a sensitive manner.

EQUALITY OF OPPORTUNITY IN PRACTICE LEARNING

30

It is vitally important that all students have equal opportunities. You will know from your professional practice that equal opportunities is not about "treating everyone the same". It's more about anti-oppressive practice, recognising and responding to diversity and addressing unique and specific needs.

The main starting point is to recognise that all students are individuals with diverse backgrounds and situations. In your initial meetings with students, you need to consider with the student whether they have any specific requirements.

Some of the individual situations which have an impact on assessment are outlined in this chapter. However, it is important to remember that this is not an exhaustive list and there may be other circumstances which create specific requirements in terms of practice learning. The key to effective practice learning is to ensure that you see every student as a unique individual with their own specific needs and requirements and that you seek to address any specific requirements in facilitating learning opportunities, choosing appropriate assessment methods and all other aspects of the placement experience.

Students with Disabilities/Health Needs

Where a student has a disability, you need to negotiate with them as soon as possible what support they will require and how the learning opportunities provided and assessment methods to be utilised may need to be adapted (eg: the provision of case studies in large print or braille). You may need to ensure that certain equipment or facilities are available for students with disabilities or specific health needs. For example, you may need to ensure a fridge is available for a student to keep medication in, that a quiet room is available for a student to take a short rest, that an amplified telephone is available etc. Staff at the University should be able to advise and assist with this. Some students may have a personal support worker or enabler to assist them. The student will be able to advise you about the extent of their role. All of this shows how important placement planning and preparation is. You will also need to discuss with the student how much information (if any) about their health and support needs should be shared with others in the setting.

Students have the right to choose whether to disclose that they have a disability. However, often Universities provide students with guidance, encouraging disclosure to ensure that their needs can be addressed. The Best Practice Guide: disabled social work students and placements, produced in 2005 by the University of Hull states:

"Disclosure should be made to the course and the placement as early as possible. Disclosure of disability is a matter of personal choice and it is important that you consider the valid reasons for and against disclosure. However, if your course or placement is not aware of your disability, it may not be able to make reasonable adjustments to help you…."

(Wray et al 2005:6)

The term 'reasonable adjustments' in the above quotation is important. Under equality legislation, social work students are legally entitled to expect reasonable adjustments, both in the University and on placement. This means that placement providers, supervisors and practice educators will need to be creative in the learning and assessment methods utilised and make reasonable adjustments to meet the needs of students.

The following checklist is helpful in considering effective practice education with students with disabilities and specific health needs:

- ✓ Encourage and value disabled students
- ✓ Negotiate with everyone in the placement setting to maximise the opportunities available to the student
- ✓ Ask the student what will best help them
- ✓ Familiarise yourself with the role of the support worker/enabler (if appropriate) and ensure that everyone involved in the assessment understands the role
- ✓ Ensure that the student has access to any necessary technology and equipment
- ✓ Challenge any barrier within yourself or your agency which blocks the student's ability to function, participate and develop
- ✗ Don't patronise

(Adapted from Moss, Marsh and Stockman 1997)

Students with Dyslexia

Guidance to legislation, such as the Equality Act, makes it clear that dyslexia is covered in definitions of disability. We have, however, chosen to look at this issue separately as it is an area which many practice educators and supervisors struggle with. In addition, many students who have dyslexia do not see their condition as a disability and may not raise it as an issue with you at the start of the placement, unless you ask a specific question about it.

The impact of dyslexia varies greatly from one individual to another, but may include:
- difficulties with spelling
- slow reading and comprehension
- slow disjointed handwriting
- miscopying
- difficulties with presenting ideas on paper
- difficulties with memory
- difficulties with processing information
- difficulties with organisation and time management
- difficulties in expressing ideas orally
- difficulties in pronouncing unfamiliar words
- problems with motor skills

Many people with dyslexia develop specific coping mechanisms to address these issues. Sometimes these coping mechanisms translate effectively into the placement environment, sometimes they don't. It's important to discuss what best meets the needs of students with dyslexia with them at an early stage and keep this under review. Examples of things practice educators can do to assist students with dyslexia include:

- producing written material on cream or coloured paper
- using fonts such as Arial or Comic Sans which are generally seen as more accessible
- repeating instructions and requirements a number of times, especially early in the placement
- providing information in the form of mind maps or flow charts
- devising prompt sheets
- supporting students to access appropriate technology and software (eg: voice activated word processing)

The key thing, as with all situations, is to ask students about what would best suit their needs. Think creatively and be willing to adopt a flexible approach.

Students from Discriminated Against Groups

People from discriminated against groups, such as black people and people with disabilities, are likely to have had negative experiences in education. *"People from discriminated against groups are used to having their knowledge and experience devalued and disbelieved, both individually and communally."* (ILPS 1993)

Students from discriminated against groups may therefore have specific requirements in terms of practice learning. For example, practice educators should take into account the negative, previous experiences that the student has had in ensuring they create a safe environment for learning and assessment. Practice educators should also understand that the fear of prejudice and discrimination may mean that the student is not open in their exchanges with the practice educator, which may inhibit their performance.

Worryingly, research about Black African students experiences of placements indicates that students experienced institutional racism on a range of levels (Bartoli, Kennedy and Tedam 2008). The experiences reported by students identified that they were subjected to stereotyping, mistrusted and patronised.

The value of mentoring for learners from discriminated against groups has long been recognised and some social work programmes have mentoring schemes for students from discriminated against groups – such as students with disabilities, black students and gay students. Find out if this is the case for any programme you are working with and ensure that every student (not just those you consider to be from a discriminated against group) knows how to access any mentoring scheme.

Many agencies have support groups or networks available for staff from discriminated against groups – find out what is available in your agency and again, ensure that all students are aware of any groups and support networks.

Students who Lack Confidence

Students may lack confidence for a range of reasons. For example, students who have not been supported through continual constructive feedback on their work, may lack confidence in their work.

Students who lack confidence will need encouragement to work in partnership with their practice educator. Effective planning and ground rules will be especially important to ensure that students who lack confidence are clear about what exactly they need to do to demonstrate capability. Practice educators will also need to provide regular constructive feedback which builds on the student's confidence.

Cultural Needs

It is important to consider and address any specific cultural needs that students might have. For example, is there a room which could be used by a student who needs to pray? If your service has set holidays around Christmas and Easter, remember that these are Christian festivals; students may want to have leave for other cultural festivals such as Eid or Hanukkah. During festivals which might involve fasting, you may need to adapt working hours. Make sure you discuss cultural requirements with students.

As previously stated, this list is not exhaustive. Students may have specific needs for a range of other reasons, such as:

- Negative previous experiences of learning and/or assessment
- Limited experience
- Care commitments

In addition, some students may belong to more than one of the groups outlined in this section. For example, students with dyslexia may also lack confidence (perhaps as a direct result of their dyslexia).

IN SUMMARY

It is vital to negotiate with students on an individual basis about their particular needs and requirements. Remember though that students may not always articulate their needs and any difficulties they encounter due to apprehension or stigma. Be clear that you will not discriminate against students on the basis of any specific requirements.

31 ETHICAL ISSUES IN PRACTICE LEARNING

A number of ethical dilemmas can arise during practice learning opportunities.

Intrusion

One of the most difficult issues is that of intrusion into the privacy of service users and carers. Practice educators and students should discuss this in detail as part of the planning process. This issue has been recognised for some time now. As far back as 1992, CCETSW advised those responsible for assessing social work students as follows:

"When negotiating ………. the selection of methods for gathering evidence, the assessor must make certain that the methods selected do not intrude on the rights of [service users] and their carers."

There may be some situations where, for example, direct observation of practice may be overly intrusive. It must always be remembered that a service user's consent for observation needs to be obtained and that they have the right to withdraw this consent at any point.

Asking a student to explore the issues surrounding service users and carers rights and the tensions that arise in terms of the student's placement may be a helpful strategy in terms of this. It aids the practice educator in terms of exploring ethics in assessment and will also help the student to develop and demonstrate their capability in terms of values and ethics in practice.

Confidentiality

Service users and carers have a right to confidentiality. This can be inadvertently breached in the assessment process. It is vital that students and practice educators work to ensure that confidentiality is upheld.

The University should provide guidelines on the methods of anonymising evidence to ensure confidentiality is maintained. Explanations should be given to service users and others involved in the placement about the methods used to uphold confidentiality. The way a student approaches confidentiality in their placement will provide you with evidence of the student's practice and understanding of ethical issues and dilemmas in this area.

Students also have the right to confidentiality in terms of their practice learning experience. You must store assessment documentation and portfolios securely. Don't leave them on your desk where they can be seen by others. Again, the University should provide guidelines in relation to confidentiality for students.

The Data Protection Act (1998) covers the way in which personal and sensitive information should be handled. You will, no doubt, be familiar with this in terms of your work practice, but don't forget that it also applies to your work as a placement supervisor or practice educator.

Quality of Service Provided to Service Users

It is vital to remember that the primary focus in all situations must be the quality of the service provided to the service user and not the student's placement.

Commitment to service quality can be lost where students and practice educators are overly enthusiastic about the learning and assessment processes. It is important that the student and practice educator always check the service user's willingness with them at all stages of the practice learning process.

Remember too that your role as a practice educator is about the safeguarding of standards of practice. Your role is not about "getting the student through" rather it's about "is this student capable and able to practice effectively?"

Ultimately practice education is about safeguarding the long term future of the profession. You must be willing to fail a student if necessary:

"Practice educators have an individual and collective responsibility to ensure that qualifying social workers are competent to practice. This requires a rigorous assessment of competence and a willingness to contribute to the ongoing development of social work education at a local and national level."

(NOPT 2013)

IN SUMMARY

A range of challenges and ethical issues can arise during practice learning opportunities. All social work practitioners should practice ethically. These principles should be translated into the practice teaching role.

KEY LEARNING POINTS

- The professional value base must be integrated into all aspects of practice learning
- There are marked power differentials in the range of relationships in any practice learning opportunity
- Where power dynamics are not discussed and addressed, a student is likely to feel disempowered – this will have a major impact on the success of the practice learning opportunity
- Practice educators need to address student's individual needs in order to ensure equal opportunities in practice learning
- A number of ethical issues and dilemmas occur in practice learning. Practice educators need to be aware of these and work ethically at all times.

WHEN THINGS "GO WRONG"

Practice learning is generally a positive experience for all involved. If the guidance provided in the previous sections of this guide is followed, then problems are unlikely to occur. However, occasionally problems of various kinds do occur. This final section considers the way in which any problems can be explored and addressed, and offers guidance on working with failing and marginal students.

32 — ADDRESSING PROBLEMS IN PRACTICE LEARNING

Practice learning is generally a very positive experience for everyone involved. However, a range of problems or difficult issues can occur. It is easy to see the potential for conflict or other difficulties if you consider the number of people potentially involved in practice learning.

It is not possible in a guide of this kind to consider all of the potential problems which can occur in practice learning. Rather, we will consider, in general, situations in practice learning which could be thought of as 'problematic'.

It is common in such situations for the practice educator and placement supervisor to question themselves. It is always helpful to begin with an examination of the practice learning and assessment process and your role in this, but beware of "blaming yourself". This said, you may find it useful to work through the following questions. These are designed to help you identify the root of the "problem" and then to try and identify a strategy to deal with the situation, perhaps designing a new, more effective, way of managing the practice learning opportunity or working with the student.

- **Power and Powerlessness**
  Have you addressed this with the student in a way that would enable them to get the most out of placement and demonstrate competence? See Chapter 29.

- **Placement Preparation**
  Have you prepared everyone fully for the practice learning process? See Chapter 7.

- **Agreements and Curriculums**
  Is the learning agreement clear about what is expected? Was this negotiated clearly with the student? Do you have a clear set of ground rules? Is there a clear assessment plan? Is there a comprehensive curriculum? Have all of these been kept under review and updated as necessary? See Chapters 8 and 13.

- **The Assessment Process**
  Have you assessed the student holistically? Have you considered the common sources of error in the assessment of competence? See Chapter 26.

- **Feedback**
  Have you given clear, constructive feedback to the student throughout the practice learning opportunity? See Chapter 25.

- **Specific Needs**
  Have you clearly considered any specific needs the student has and addressed these in the practice learning opportunity? See Chapter 30.

- **Partnership**
  Have you worked in a way which encourages the student to take responsibility for their own learning, giving the student support where required?

- **Opportunities**
  Has the student benefited from sufficient opportunities to demonstrate competence?

- **Assessment Methods**
  Have you used a sufficient range of assessment methods to enable the student to demonstrate their practice? See Chapter 23.

- **The Context of Assessment**
  Do you and the student fully understand the assessment criteria? Have you sought advice and support from relevant people?

- **Roles and Responsibilities**
  Is everyone's role and responsibility clear? In off site arrangements, are robust arrangements in place in terms of the three way relationship (between student, practice educator and placement supervisor)?

- **Timing is vital**
  Where there are any difficulties in a placement, it is vital that these are raised at the earliest opportunity. Schaub and Dalrymple (2011) quote practice educators who have worked in difficult situations saying *"speak early and honestly"* and *"Don't ignore it. You've got to address it early"*. Remember if you try to ignore problems and sweep them 'under the carpet', the problems don't go away; they simply pile up and can trip everyone up later in the placement.

IN SUMMARY

Reflecting on your practice in situations where things are "going wrong" in practice learning can help to identify a solution and an action plan for getting things back on track.

WORKING WITH STUDENTS IN FAILING AND MARGINAL SITUATIONS

Unfortunately, on some occasions students do fail to progress and demonstrate capability at the required standard. In such situations, generally students fall into one of two categories:

- Marginal – essentially a marginal student is one who may be referred to as "borderline". If by the mid point of the placement a practice educator isn't able to positively answer the question "is this student on target to pass the placement?" with some confidence, the student could be considered marginal.

- Failing – where students are failing, it should be clearer to identify than when a student is marginal. It may be clear that the student is a long way from demonstrating capability or in fact the student may be practicing in a way which directly contravenes the required standards of practice.

Marsh et al (2005) state that concerns about failing students generally relate to:

- Poor communication and interpersonal skills
- Lack of interest and failure to participate in practice learning
- Persistent lateness
- Lack of personal insight
- Lack of insight into professional boundaries

In our experience, failing students usually exhibit a combination of these characteristics.

When you feel that a student is either failing or marginal, it is worth going through the checklist contained in Chapter 32 and identifying any issues impeding on the student's development. It is also important to consider your standards and whether you are assessing at the correct level. Sometimes, practice educators are looking for capability at a higher level than is required – always keep this under review. Refer to the specific capability statements of the PCF at the level the student is working at to ensure you are looking for the right level of capability.

Procedures

Universities will all have concerns procedures which come into play when a student is identified as failing or marginal. Each programme will differ but as a general requirement where there are concerns, these procedures should be invoked as soon as possible. Most concerns procedures involve one (or both) of the following:

- *Concerns Meeting and Action Planning*
  A meeting will be held involving the student, their tutor, the practice educator and the placement supervisor (where relevant). The concerns and each person's perspective on these will be discussed and an action plan outlining how the concerns will be addressed should be drawn up in agreement with all parties.

- *Second Opinion Practice Educator*
  The rules and requirements for the DipSW said that where a student was deemed to be failing or marginal, a second opinion practice educator must become involved. Whilst this is not a requirement within the social work degree, many programmes maintained the principles of second opinion processes. Again, all University programmes vary in their use of second opinion practice educators. However, the basic process is for an experienced practice educator to go into the practice learning environment and do a 'snap shot' assessment of the student in order to offer a second opinion. The original practice educator continues to work with the student. Since so much power is invested in the practice educator role, the second opinion process is really about ensuring that this is not being misused.

  "The principle of obtaining a second opinion for students is undoubtedly a good one, in the interests of fairness and objectivity, to ensure an accurate assessment is made."

  (Buchanan and McMullan 2000)

  You must ensure that as a practice educator, you are familiar with the procedures in place in the programme you are working with. Ensure that these are discussed and agreed in the pre placement meeting and that everyone, including the student, is confident about the procedures and understands in what circumstances they might be instigated.

The Benefit of the Doubt?

Instigating concerns procedures is a task fraught with difficult emotions. It is perhaps for this reason that although practice educators have concerns, sometimes from an early stage of a placement, they delay instigating concerns procedures until as late as possible or (even more dangerous) don't instigate the procedures at all. We have already considered how it is dangerous to give students the benefit of the doubt. Most people would agree that it is dangerous to pass a student who does not progress to the required level, not least because this:

- Does not protect the interests of the public and puts clients who will be in their care at risk
- Has detrimental effects for the profession and standards we seek to uphold
- Means we fail in our duty of care to safeguard the safety of those we serve

(Marsh et al 2005)

It is absolutely vital therefore that:

"if you are thinking of giving the student the benefit of the doubt, then you should firstly consider whether it is in the best interests of ... your clients, the student, subsequent Practice Educators and professionals as a whole."

(Duffy 2004:9)

The problems with giving students the benefit of the doubt also potentially sets up a student to fail when they might be able to develop considerably with appropriate action planning. The best advice is to discuss any concerns with students as early as possible and to instigate concerns procedures at an early stage. Concerns procedures should be viewed positively – action planning and second opinion processes can really support students to develop their practice and in many cases where concerns procedures are instigated, students go on to successfully pass the placement. For those students who still do not progress, programmes will have a range of "exit routes" which they can support students into.

Recognising and Addressing Emotional Issues

If there are concerns about a student's level of capability, then both the student and practice educator will be dealing with a range of difficult emotions. These are likely to affect the relationship between the student and practice educator, and they can certainly lead to a lot of sleepless nights.

This illustrates why it is important for students and practice educators to receive additional support when concerns are being addressed. The University should be able to advise on where the student can obtain support from. The agency which employs the practice educator (more often than not the placement provider) should be able to offer support to practice educators. Practice educator support groups can also be a useful source of support during these experiences.

It also shows that practice educators and supervisors must be aware of their own practice, follow good practice guidelines and work within programme requirements. If a person feels under pressure, the human reaction is "fight or flight". Often therefore students facing the prospect of failing a placement will make accusations about the practice educator or infer that there were problems with their placement. The importance of vigilant recording is therefore highlighted in such situations.

Possible Outcomes

As stated, one of the outcomes that can result from following concerns procedures is that the student can develop considerably and go on to the pass the placement. However, in some circumstances, students do fail to reach the required standard by the end of a placement. Various options are then possible:

- The student may undertake a repeat placement in a new practice leaning environment – this may give then the opportunity to develop further and to ultimately pass the course.

- Sometimes, students are given the opportunity to transfer onto a related academic degree which does not involve assessed practice – such as a degree in one of the social sciences.

- Sometimes students defer a year, obtain additional experience and repeat the failed placement if not the whole year.

Sometimes, students just aren't cut out for social work, at least at that stage in their lives and failing a student should not be considered a "disaster" for their future. Indeed, if a student were passed when they were not ready to practice social work, they could be "set up to fail" in their future. There are potentially a number of positive outcomes for students. Don't feel under pressure to pass a student who isn't capable because of a fear about their future. Indeed, I worked with one student where I recommended a fail – he took some time out to gain additional experience and returned to the course later, ultimately achieving the qualification. He still writes to me from time to time to say, whilst it didn't feel like it at the time, I did him what he describes as a "huge favour" in not "sending me into practice when I wasn't ready."

Good Practice in Working with Failing and Marginal Students

Marsh et al (2005) provide the following really useful framework for working with students in failing and marginal situations.

We suggest:

- Early exploration and intervention with the student eg: ask why they appear to lack interest
- Fairness. Avoid making assumptions and jumping to conclusions
- Clear articulation of expectations
- Prompt removal of obstacles to allow facilitation of progress
- Negotiation of learning opportunities

If the problems do not resolve, you need to:

- Give formal written feedback at an early stage
- Arrange a meeting between the student, practice educator and tutor
- Develop an action plan agreed by all parties
- Arrange regular review of progress and feedback meetings
- Give the student every opportunity and support to progress
- Recognise that some students need to fail

(adapted from Marsh et al 2005:8)

Getting Support

Practice educators working with failing and marginal students report feeling very isolated as they go through this difficult experience (eg: Basnett and Sheffield 2010). It is vital that if you are involved in any difficult situation in practice learning, you seek appropriate support to avoid feelings of isolation.

IN SUMMARY

Most students progress well in practice learning environments and pass the placement. However, sometimes students will fail. This is an emotionally draining time for students and practice educators. Practice educators should seek support from a variety of sources.

KEY LEARNING POINTS

- Problems are unlikely to occur if practice learning processes are carefully followed and good practice is seen as a priority
- Where problems do occur, the practice educator should reflect on the situation and seek to find a solution
- Working with failing and marginal students is emotionally draining but practice educators must be willing to fail a student where necessary in order to safeguard the profession

CPD FOR PRACTICE EDUCATION

Continual professional development is important for all professionals. Practice educators and placement supervisors need to model a commitment to continuing development to students who are at an earlier stage of their professional journey.

Practice educators, and those placement supervisors who are registered, will need to meet the CPD Standards for their ongoing registration and their role in practice education should be included in this.

This section explores aspects of continual professional development in relation to practice education.

LINKS TO PEPS — DOMAIN D

34 AN INTRODUCTION TO PROFESSIONAL DEVELOPMENT

In recent years the vital importance of continual professional development (often referred to as CPD) has received increasing attention in the health and social care sector. In 2007 a joint position statement on continuing professional development for health and social care practitioners was published. This joint position statement was a collaboration between seventeen key organisations in health and social care including the Royal College of Nursing and Unison. This statement makes clear that *"CPD is fundamental to the development of all health and social care practitioners and is the mechanism through which high quality... care is identified, maintained and developed"* (RCN 2007:2). The connection between CPD and high quality practice has also been highlighted in UK Government documents and Regulatory Body documents (for example see the Department of Health 2004 and 2007c, Welsh Assembly Government 2010).

Benefits of continual professional development

Where health and social care practitioners take an active approach to their own professional development there are a range of acknowledged benefits (Thompson 1996). For example:

Increased job satisfaction: Learning can be stimulating and rewarding and can improve job satisfaction.

Improved practice: Where a practitioner develops their knowledge and skills this will lead to improved practice and better outcomes for service users.

Stress management and burnout prevention: Social workers operate in complex and demanding situations. This can lead to stress and ultimately "burnout". Engaging in effective continual professional development can assist in avoiding compassion fatigue and burnout. This has been recognised in a range of studies, including international research on standards in social work practice (IFSW 2010).

Recognition of change: Continuing to learn and develop can help social workers to understand the basis of change in the profession and the health and social care sector more generally. This will enable them to adapt to change more effectively.

Self-awareness: Being "self-aware" is an important aspect of best practice. Continual professional development will help practitioners to develop their self awareness.

Improved relationships with colleagues and other agencies: Partnership working becomes easier and more enjoyable when workers can take opportunities to learn from other professionals about their roles, perspectives and ideas.

Career development: Workers who take pro-active approaches to their own development may be more likely in some organisations to develop their careers further as more opportunities to enlarge or enrich roles may be offered to workers who are perceived by the organisation as open to change and development.

Professional development and practice learning are linked in two main ways:

- Being involved in practice learning provides opportunities for social workers to learn and develop their own social work practice.
- Practice educators and others involved in practice learning need to continually develop their practice to improve the provision of quality practice learning.

Practice educators will be registered as social workers and a number of supervisors may also be registered social workers. As such, they will need to meet the CPD requirements of the HCPC. Their role in practice education will form part of the scope of their role and therefore they should reflect on how they have:

- Drawn on their practice education experiences to develop their social work practice.
- Developed their practice as a practice educator / placement supervisor.

IN SUMMARY

CPD is vital for every social worker. Involvement in practice learning can be used as a CPD activity. Practice educators should also consider how they can enhance and develop their own practice education skills through a range of CPD activities.

35 CONTINUING DEVELOPMENT AS A PRACTICE EDUCATOR

As someone responsible for facilitating the learning of others you should recognise effective ways to enhance your own learning and development. Perhaps the most important aspect is to take a critically reflective approach to your own experiences as a practice educator, reflecting on what you have learnt and how you can apply this learning to improve your practice in the future. You can draw on a range of evidence to inform your reflections including:

- Feedback from the student and others involved in the practice learning provision (including both formal and informal feedback)
- The result of QAPL evaluations (see page 48)
- Feedback from the Practice Assessment Panel on the practice learning documentation
- Research findings and other reading

Reflecting on the feedback you have received is likely to be one of the most effective ways to consider your practice and improve it for the future. Other CPD activities which may be useful to you in maintaining effective performance as a practice educator include:

Training: A range of training opportunities are available for practice educators. Often these are arranged by local partnerships. Look out for training which you may find useful in your role as a practice educator but also take a proactive approach to training. If you feel that you have a specific learning need which could be met through training of some kind then inform the practice learning co-ordinator in our area – they may well be able to organise some training to meet these needs.

Assessment: As a practice educator you will understand that assessment and learning are intrinsically linked. There are many opportunities for practice educators to be assessed formally – either as part of a local programme or qualification or as part of a local quality assurance process. Being directly observed in providing supervision might be anxiety provoking – but as a practice educator I find it one of the most useful learning experiences available to me and I arrange to be formally observed in practice every couple of years.

Mentoring: In Ancient Greek mythology when Odysseus went to Troy he left Mentor to be the trusted friend and advisor to his son. Since then the word mentoring has been used to describe a relationship where one person who is more experienced than another takes on a role to assist, support and advise the other. Traditionally people have sought informal mentors. For example, when a person takes on the role of a practice educator for the first time they may approach someone who they know is experienced in the role and whose practice they respect to ask questions and sound out ideas etc. Many organisations have started to recognise the value of mentoring and have established formal mentoring systems for those new to practice education. Very often because of the skills they have, practice educators are asked to mentor other staff – for example those new to the team or newly qualified workers. Being a mentor as well as having a mentor can be a useful CPD activity.

Involvement in HEI activities: Universities are generally very keen to have social work practitioners and practice educators involved in a range of ways in their programme design, delivery and evaluation. Delivering presentations to students; involvement in skills workshops; attending quality assurance meetings and interviewing of students are all useful opportunities for learning and development.

Journals: Articles about practice learning and social work education are included in a range of the professional journals. The Journal of Practice Teaching and Learning is a specialist journal which covers practice education in social work and health.

Membership of professional bodies: The National Organisation for Practice Teaching (NOPT) is a voluntary organisation which works to represent the interests of practice educators through consultation with the major bodies involved in social work education. Membership is open to all individuals. The organisation has an informative website and facilitates a members forum. Many practice educators find membership is useful in maintaining their knowledge about practice education. Membership of other professional bodies such as the British Association of Social Workers and the College of Social Work is often useful to practice educators too.

Attending practice assessment panels: Practice educators are generally invited to be part of practice assessment panels. Practice educators can learn a great deal from attending panels and reading student reports. Do take the opportunity to attend panels and other quality assurance meetings at local Universities.

Attending support groups: Many organisations hold support groups for practice educators and placement supervisors, as do many universities. Learning from the experiences and activities of others is particularly helpful for those new to practice learning provision.

Maintaining currency in experience: In order to maintain your skills and knowledge it is important to continue to work with students on a regular basis. As you will know the less frequently you use your skills in anything the more "rusty" they become. Practice educators probably learn more from working with students than they do from anything else. Regularly supporting students in practice and reflecting on these experiences in probably the best way to maintain and improve your skills.

Extension of skills through job enrichment / enlargement: Concepts of job enlargement and enrichment are drawn from Porter et al's model (1982) which considers job characteristics and associated learning. The model explores the importance of job satisfaction and the way that different work roles motivate people in different ways and therefore prompt learning at different levels. When people have been in a particular role for some time, their satisfaction with the role may reduce and their performance may be adversely affected. The model describes how this can be addressed by changing jobs either through enlargement or enrichment:

Enlargement means extending the scope of the job by combining two or more jobs into one, giving greater variety and a more 'holistic' feel.

Enrichment means people having more responsibility for setting their own pace, deciding their own methods and passing on their skills to others – resulting in greater autonomy.

Those involved in practice learning could be seen as experiencing enlargement and enrichment in relation to their usual role. Those people who have been involved in practice education for some time could enrich this role by looking at acting as a mentor to others or becoming involved in other aspects of social work education.

IN SUMMARY

You can make use of a range of methods to enhance your learning and development. After all everything can be a learning opportunity, but remember it's not what you do - it's the way that you do it. Taking an open and reflective approach to your practice is the most important way to ensure that you continually improve your performance as a practice educator. Learning is a two way process and ensuring that you model a commitment to continual professional development is probably the most effective way of ensuring that a student becomes a practitioner who takes a proactive approach to continuing their development throughout their career.

KEY LEARNING POINTS

- CPD is vital for all professionals
- Involvement in practice education can be used as a CPD activity
- A range of CPD activities are available to support practice educators to continually improve their practice
- To maintain currency in terms of skills and knowledge it is important to work with students on a regular basis

REFERENCES

Akubuilo, F. (2012) *Holistic Assessment of Students Learning Outcome.* Journal of Education and Practice, 3(12) p. 56-60.

Atherton, S. (2006) *Putting Group Learning into Practice in Social Work Education.* (Leeds) Skills for Care in partnership with the West Midlands Learning Resource Network.

Barcham, C. (2012) *Child Protection Standards and the College of Social Work.* Presentation to BASPCAN 8th Congress 2012. Queen's University Belfast.

Bartoli, A., Kennedy, S. and Tedam, P. (2008) *Practice Learning: Who is failing to adjust? Black African Student experience of practice learning in a social work setting.* Journal of Practice Teaching and Learning 8(2) p. 75-90.

Basnett, F. and Sheffield, D. (2010) *The Impact of Social Work Student Failures upon Practice Educators.* British Journal of Social Work, 40(7) p. 2119-2136.

BASW (2012) *The Code of Ethics for Social Work: Statement of Principles.* (Birmingham) British Association of Social Workers.

Biggs, J. (1999) *Teaching for Quality Learning at University.* (Buckingham) Society for Research into Higher Development.

Billington, D. (1996) *Seven Characteristics of Highly Effective Adult Learning Programs.* New Horizons for Learning – available online at: www.newhorizons.org/lifelong/workplace/billington.htm (accessed 12.1.08)

Bogg, D. and Challis, M. (2013) *Evidencing CPD- A Guide to Building Your Social Work Portfolio.* (St Albans) Critical Publishing.

Bolton, G. (2001) *Reflective Practice.* (London) Sage.

Brown, J.S., Collins, A. and Duguid, S. (1989) *Situated Cognition and the Culture of Learning.* Educational Researcher, 18(1) p. 32-42.

Brown, K. and Rutter, L. (2006) *Critical Thinking for Social Work.* (Exeter) Learning Matters.

Buchanan, J. and McMullan, P. (2000) *A matter of opinion.* Available online at: www.communitycare.co.uk/Articles/2000/11/02/28653/a-matter-of-opinion.html (accessed 21.1.08)

Burns, R. (1995) *The Adult Learner at Work.* (Sydney) Business and Professional Publishers.

CCETSW (1992) *National Vocational Qualifications in Care: Notes on Assessment and Guidance.* (London) CCETSW.

Dahlgren, L.O., Eriksson, B.E., Gyllenhammar, H., Korkeila, M., and Saaf-Rothoff, A. (2006) *To be and to have a critical friend in medical teaching.* Journal of Medical Education, 40 (1) p. 5-6.

Danbury, H. (1994) *Teaching Practical Social Work.* Third Edition. (Aldershot) Arena Press.

Department of Health (2004) *NHS knowledge and skills framework (NHS KSF) and the development review process.* (London) HMSO.

Department of Health (2007) *Continuing Professional Development.* Available online at: http://webarchive.nationalarchives.gov.uk/+/www.dh.gov.uk/en/Managingyourorganisation/Workforce/Educationtraininganddevelopment/ (accessed 10.1.12.)

De Shazer, S. (1985) *Keys to Solution in Brief Therapy.* (New York) Norton.

Doel, M. and Shardlow, S. (1998) *The New Social Work Practice: Exercises and Activities.* (Aldershot) Ashgate.

Doel, M. and Shardlow, S. (2005) *Modern Social Work Practice : teaching and learning in Practice settings.* (Aldershot) Ashgate.

Duffy, K. (2004) *Failing Students: Should You Give them the Benefit of the Doubt?* NMC News, No 8. July 2004.

Festinger, L. (1957) *A Theory of Cognitive Dissonance.* (Stanford) Stanford University Press.

Fletcher, S. (1992) *Competence Based Assessment Techniques.* (London) Kogan Page.

Foord, K.A. and Haar, J.M. (2008) *Professional Learning Communities: An Implementation Guide and Toolkit.* (New York) Eye on Education.

General Social Care Council (2002) *Guidance on the Assessment of Practice in the Workplace.* (London) GSCC.

Honey, P. and Mumford, A. (1982) *Manual of Learning Styles.* (Maidenhead) Peter Honey Publications.

Honey, P. and Mumford, A. (1986) *Using Your Learning Styles.* (Maidenhead) Peter Honey Publications.

Houghton, W. (2004) *Engineering Subject Centre Guide.* Available online at: www.engsc.ac.uk/er/theory/learning.asp (accessed 18.1.08)

Huba, M.E. and Freed, J.E. (2000) *Learner-centred assessment on college campuses.* (Boston) Allyn and Bacon.

Hughes, R. (2006) *From Solos to Symphonies: Orchestrating Learning through Collaboration.* Compus contact – available on line at: www.compact.org/20th/read/from_solos_to_symphonies (accessed 28.12.2007)

IFSW (2010) *Social Work Standards Meeting Human Rights.* (Berlin) International Federation of Social Workers, European Region.

IFSW (2013) *Update on the review process of the Definition of Social Work.* Available online at: www.ifsw.org/news/update-on-the-review-process. (accessed 21.7.13)

IFSW and IASSW (2000) *International Definition of Social Work.* Available online at: www.ifsw.org/policies/definitions-of-social-work. (accessed 21.7.13)

Inner London Probation Service (1995) *Working with Difference: A Positive and Practical Guide to Anti-Discriminatory Practice Teaching.* (London) I.L.P.S.

Kadushin, A. (1976) *Supervision in Social Work.* (New York) Columbia University Press.

Kejawa, I. (2010) *Education: Leadership in Positive Ways.* (Pennsylvania) Red Lead Press.

Killian, J. and Todnem, G. (1991) *Reflective judgment concepts of justification and their relationship to age and education.* Journal of Applied Developmental Psychology, 2(2) p. 89-116.

Knowles (1970) *The Modern Practice of Adult Education: Andragogy versus Pedagogy.* (New York) Association Press.

Knowles, M. (1978) *The Adult Learner: A Negotiated Species.* 2nd edition (Houston) Gulf Publishing.

Kolb, D.A. (1984) *Experiential Learning: Experience as the Source of Learning and Development.* (New Jersey) Prentice-Hall.

Laming (2003) *The Victoria Climbié Inquiry.* (London) Command Paper 5730.

Lave, J. and Wenger, E. (1990) *Situated Learning: Legitimate Peripheral Participation.* (Cambridge) Cambridge University Press.

Lawson, H. (2013) *Newly Qualified Social Workers and the PCF: a survival guide.* Available online at http://www.communitycare.co.uk/articles/31/08/2012/118488/newly-qualified-social-workers-and-the-pcf-a-survival-guide.htm (accessed 8.7.13).

Lester, S. (1999) *From map-reader to map-maker: approaches to moving beyond knowledge and competence.* In O'Reilly, D, Cunningham, L. and Lester, S. (eds) Developing the Capable Practitioner. (London) Kogan Page.

Maclean, S. (2007) *Developing Partnership Working in Social Work Education: Where Are We Now?* Skills for Care West Midlands.

Marsh, S., Cooper, K., Jordan, G., Merrett, S., Scammell, J. and Clark, V. (2005) *Assessment of Students in Health and Social Care: Managing Failing Students in Practice.* Making Practice Based Learning Work. Available on line at: www.practicebasedlearning.org/resources/materials/docs/failing%20 students-%20final%20version%2022%20Nov.pdf (accessed on 21.1.08)

Marton, F. and Saljo, R. (1976) *On Qualitative Differences in Learning: 1. Outcome and Process.* British Journal of Educational Psychology p. 46, 4-11.

McClure, P. (2002) *Reflection in Practice. Making Practice Based Learning Work.* (Ulster) University of Ulster.

Mehrabian, A. and Ferris, I. (1967) *Inference of Attitudes from Non Verbal Communication in Two Channels.* The Journal of Counselling Psychology Vol. 31 p. 248-252.

Morrison, T. (2005) *Staff Supervision in Social Care: Making a Real Difference for Staff and Service Users.* (Brighton) Pavilion Publishing Ltd.

Moss, B., Marsh, J. and Stockman, S. (1997) *Disability Issues in Social Work Training and Practice.* (Wrexham) Prospects Publications Ltd.

Mullins, L. (2005: 7th edition) *Management and Organisational Behaviour.* (London) Kogan Page.

Munro, E. (2011) *The Munro Review of Child Protection: Final Report. A child-centred system.* (London) Department for Education: The Stationery Office.

National Organisation for Practice Teaching (2013) *Code of Practice for Practice Educators.* NOPT. Available online at www.nopt.org (accessed 3.7.13)

National Organisation for Practice Teaching (2006) *Good Practice Guide for Placements for the Social Work Degree* (Draft). Available online at: www.nopt.org (accessed 1.12.07)

O'Grady, G. (2004) *Holistic assessment and problem based learning.* 5th Asia Pacific Conference on PBL. 16-17 March 2004. p.13.

Porter, L., Bingley, G. and Steers, R. (1982) *Motivation and Work Behaviour.* (New York) McGraw Hill.

RMIT University Study and Learning Centre (2007) *Reflective Journal Help.* Available online at: www.dlsweb.rmit.edu.au/lsu/content2_Assessment Tasks/assess_pdf/Reflective%20journal.pdf (accessed 12.1.08)

Rogers, C. (1980) *Freedom to Learn for the 80s.* (New York) Free Press.

Rowntree, D. (1987) *Assessing Students: How shall we know them?* (2nd revised edition). (London) Kogan Page.

Royal College of Nursing (2007) *Joint position statement: A joint statement on continuing professional development for health and social care practitioners.* (London) RCN.

Schaub, J. and Dalrymple, R. (2011) *'She didn't seem like a social worker': Practice Educators' experiences and perceptions of assessing failing social work students on placement.* SWAP Research Report. Available online at: www.swapbox.ac.uk/1151/. (accessed 14.6.12)

Schön, D (1987) *Educating the Reflective Practitioner.* (San Francisco) Jossey Bass.

Shardlow, S. and Doel, M. (1996) *Practice Learning and Teaching.* (Basingstoke) MacMillan.

Sinclair, C. (2006) *Keeping A Reflective Journal: Reflections of a Mature Student.* Available online at: www.recordingachievement.org/downloads /100080.pdf (accessed 1.1.08)

Skills for Care (2008) *National Occupational Standards: Social Work.* Available online at www.skilsforcare.org/uk/view.asp?id=140 (accessed 20.1.08).

Social Work Task Force (2009) *Building a Safe, Confident Future: The Final Report of the Social Work Task Force.* November 2009. (London) Department for Children, Schools and Families.

Staffordshire Directorate of Social Care and Health (2005) *Practice Educator Handbook.* (Stafford) Staffordshire Directorate of Social Care and Health.

Stenhouse, L. (1975) *An Introduction to Curriculum Research and Development.* (London) Heinemann.

TCSW (2012) *Domains within the PCF. Version 1.* (London). The College of Social Work.

TCSW (2012a) *Understanding what is meant by Holistic Assessment.* (London) The College of Social Work.

TCSW (2012b) *Practice Educator Professional Standards for Social Work.* (London) The College of Social Work.

TCSW (2013) *Reforming social work qualifying education: The social work degree.* Available online at www.tcsw.org.uk/uploadedFiles/TheCollege/_CollegeLibrary/Reform_resources/ReformingSWQualifyingEducation(edref1)(1).pdf. (accessed 7.7.13).

Thompson, N. (1996) *People Skills: A Guide to Effective Practice in the Human Services.* (Hampshire) Macmillan Press Ltd.

Tisdell, E. (1995) *Creating Inclusive adult learning environments: Insights from Multi-cultural education and feminist pedagogy.* Information Series No. 361. Columbus: ERIC Clearinghouse on Adult, Career and Vocational Education, Center on Education and Training and Employment. The Ohio State University.

Tsui, M.S. (2005) *Social Work Supervision Contexts and Concepts.* (London)Sage Publications.

University of York (2000) *Facts, Feelings and Feedback: A Collaborative Model for Direct Observation* (York) University of York.

Welsh Assembly Government (2010) *Doing well, doing better: Standards for health services in Wales.* (Cardiff) Welsh Assembly Government.

Wray, J., Fell, B., Stanley, N., Manthorpe, J. and Coyne, E. (2005) *Best Practice Guide: Disabled Social Work Students and Placements.* (Hull) University of Hull.

Williams, S. and Rutter, L. (2007) *Enabling and Assessing Work Based Learning for Social Work: Supporting the Development of Professional Practice.* (Birmingham) Learn to Care.